WITHDRAWN

# Philip K. Dick

## Twayne's United States Authors Series

Warren French, Editor

*University College of Swansea, Wales*

TUSAS 533

PHILIP K. DICK
(1928–1982)
*Photo by Frank Ronan, 1981, reproduced with his permission.*

# *Philip K. Dick*

## By Douglas A. Mackey

Twayne Publishers
*A Division of G.K. Hall & Co.* • *Boston*

*Philip K. Dick*
Douglas A. Mackey

Copyright © 1988 by G.K. Hall & Co.
All rights reserved.
Published by Twayne Publishers
A Division of G.K. Hall & Co.
70 Lincoln Street
Boston, Massachusetts 02111

Copyediting supervised by Lewis DeSimone
Book production by Gabrielle B. McDonald
Book design by Barbara Anderson

Typeset in 11 pt. Garamond
by Compset, Inc., of Beverly, Massachusetts

Printed on permanent/durable acid-free paper
and bound in the United States of America

**Library of Congress Cataloging in Publication Data**

Mackey, Douglas A., 1947–
  Philip K. Dick.

  (Twayne's United States authors series ; TUSAS 533)
  Bibliography: p.
  Includes index.
  1. Dick, Philip K.—Criticism and interpretation.
I. Title.  II. Series.
PS3554.I3Z75  1988    813'.54    87-25041
ISBN 0-8057-7515-3 (alk. paper)

*To Doug Taylor*

# Contents

*About the Author*
*Preface*
*Chronology*

      *Chapter One*
      Dick's Life    1

      *Chapter Two*
      The Fifties    6

      *Chapter Three*
      The Mainstream Novels    31

      *Chapter Four*
      The Early Sixties    47

      *Chapter Five*
      The Late Sixties    82

      *Chapter Six*
      The Seventies and Eighties    108

      *Chapter Seven*
      Toward the Future    128

*Notes and References*    133
*Selected Bibliography*    137
*Index*    152

# About the Author

Douglas A. Mackey is a free-lance writer and editor living in Fairfield, Iowa. He has a Ph.D. in English from the University of Kansas. He has published articles on science fiction in *Missouri Review* and *Survey of Science Fiction Literature*. His other books include *D. H. Lawrence: The Poet Who Was Not Wrong*, *The Rainbow Quest of Thomas Pynchon*, and *Doors Into the Play* (with Sydney H. Spayde), all published by Borgo Press.

# Preface

Philip K. Dick is widely recognized as one of the finest of modern science-fiction writers. To go a step further and recognize him as one of the best modern *writers*, one would need to put aside any ideas that so-called realistic fiction is by definition superior to science fiction (or other "genre fiction"). Although Dick employs the clichés of the genre—robots, space travel, aliens, future dystopias, and so on—he does so in a consistently original way. His writing is branded with his idiosyncratic vision, which begins with a refusal to accept reality as it is ordinarily perceived, and spirals through innumerable alternate reality configurations until the reader is left helpless with astonishment. A writer who can do this as frequently and brilliantly as Dick does must be considered a major figure in twentieth-century literature.

Author of at least forty-four novels and well over a hundred short stories, as well as reams of unpublished philosophical musings, Dick is a formidable writer to cover comprehensively in a study of this length. Much has been written about him, but only one other book to date attempts to discuss all his work systematically. There are many possible angles from which to approach this rich and complex writer. My own interest is in taking Dick's central concern about the nature of reality quite seriously, and in showing how it develops throughout the novels, taken one at a time in chronological order of writing. At the same time my critiques of individual works are informed by a vision of the whole that Dick worked toward throughout his career: a synthesis of science (representing the objective world) and consciousness (the subjective). A more ambitious project for a modern novelist could scarcely be conceived.

Dick questioned whether the world that our senses perceive is real. His characters frequently suffer "reality breakdowns," where the fabric of reality dissolves around them and the whole meaning of their identity and their humanity has to be redefined. Because of this preoccupation, Dick is a thoroughly modern writer, one whom I am confident will stand with Borges and Kafka when twentieth-century literature is reviewed from a standpoint free from genre prejudices.

Dick was a fascinating personality, and much continues to be published in the way of interviews and biographical material. His life experiences and personal feelings permeated his work; it is heavily autobiographical. But he is never self-indulgent; his style never calls attention to itself. Rather, it is unostentatiously appropriate to its subject and effortlessly compelling. His characteristic irony is pervasive, but it is not of the darkest kind. Dick is endearing because he loves to laugh and share his cockeyed humor as well as his startling metaphysical insights with the reader. It is a generous attitude, one that has earned him a devoted following, whose days as a mere cult may be numbered.

I would like to thank Paul Williams, literary executor of the Philip K. Dick Estate, and Sharon Perry, Special Collections Librarian at California State University at Fullerton, for allowing me access to unpublished Dick manuscripts and letters. I trust that much of this material will someday be published, and the world will realize that Dick was a brilliant mind as well as a master entertainer.

Because Dick's works have been published in many ephemeral editions, quotations from his novels are located by chapter rather than page references.

Douglas A. Mackey

# Chronology

1928    Philip Kindred Dick born Chicago, Illinois, 16 December to Joseph Edgar Dick and Dorothy Grant Kindred Dick.

1929    Dick's twin sister Jane dies 26 January.

1933    Parents divorced.

1939    Moves with mother to Berkeley, California.

1944–1952    Works as clerk and manager in record stores.

1945    Graduates from Berkeley High School.

1948    Marries and divorces Jeanette Marlin. Enrolls at the University of California, Berkeley, dropping out after two months.

1950    Marries Kleo Apostolides.

1951    Attends writing workshops under Anthony Boucher, editor of *Fantasy and Science Fiction,* to whom he makes his first story sale, "Roog."

1952–1954    Publishes over sixty short stories in science-fiction magazines.

1953–1960    Writes twelve non-science-fiction novels, all rejected for publication at the time.

1955    *Solar Lottery* and *A Handful of Darkness* (collection).

1956    *The World Jones Made* and *The Man Who Japed.*

1957    *Eye in the Sky, The Cosmic Puppets,* and *The Variable Man* (collection).

1958    Moves with Kleo to Point Reyes Station in Marin County; meets Anne Williams Rubenstein.

1959    Divorces Kleo, marries Anne, moves into her house at Point Reyes. *Time out of Joint.*

1960    Birth of daughter Laura. *Dr. Futurity* and *Vulcan's Hammer.*

1962    *The Man in the High Castle.*

1963     *The Game-Players of Titan.* Wins Hugo Award for *The Man in the High Castle.*

1964     Moves to Berkeley; divorces Anne; meets Nancy Hackett. *The Penultimate Truth, Martian Time-Slip, The Simulacra,* and *Clans of the Alphane Moon.*

1965     *The Three Stigmata of Palmer Eldritch* and *Dr. Bloodmoney.*

1966     Marries Nancy Hackett; moves to San Rafael. *Now Wait for Last Year, The Crack in Space,* and *The Unteleported Man.*

1967     Daughter Isolde born. *The Zap Gun, Counter-Clock World, The Ganymede Takeover,* and "Faith of Our Fathers."

1968     *Do Androids Dream of Electric Sheep?*

1969     *Galactic Pot-Healer, Ubik,* and *The Preserving Machine* (collection).

1970     Breakup with Nancy. *A Maze of Death* and *Our Friends from Frolix 8.*

1971     Mysterious break-in and burglary at residence.

1972     Attempts suicide in Vancouver; enters rehabilitation center; relocates in Fullerton, California. *We Can Build You.*

1973     Marries Tessa Busby; son Christopher born.

1974     Begins having mystical experiences and writing the "Exegesis" to explain them. *Flow My Tears, the Policeman Said.*

1975     *Confessions of a Crap Artist. Flow My Tears* wins John W. Campbell Award. Profiled in *Rolling Stone.*

1976     Breakup of fifth marriage and attempted suicide. Dick moves to Santa Ana. *Deus Irae.*

1976–1979     Gregg Press publishes fourteen out-of-print Dick titles in permanent hardcover editions, with critical introductions.

1977     *The Best of Philip K. Dick* (collection) and *A Scanner Darkly.*

1978     Death of Dick's mother.

1980     *The Golden Man* (collection).

1981   *VALIS* and *The Divine Invasion.*

1982   Dick dies of a stroke, Santa Ana, 2 March. *The Trans-migration of Timothy Archer. Blade Runner* film released, and *Do Androids Dream?* reissued as *Blade Runner.*

1984   *Lies, Inc., The Man Whose Teeth Were All Exactly Alike,* and *Robots, Androids, and Mechanical Oddities* (collection).

1985   Dick's father dies. *Puttering about in a Small Land, I Hope I Shall Arrive Soon* (collection), *Ubik: The Screenplay, In Milton Lumky Territory,* and *Radio Free Albemuth.*

1986   *Humpty Dumpty in Oakland.*

1987   *The Collected Stories of Philip K. Dick* and *Mary and the Giant.*

1988   *The Broken Bubble.*

# Chapter One

# Dick's Life

Philip K. Dick may well become one of those literary figures whose life is as interesting to commentators as his works. Certainly with five marriages and innumerable other romantic relationships, Dick's life had more than its share of soap opera. Add to that the fire of a creative personality, the drugs and self-destructive tendencies, and the mystical religious experiences, and one has all the ingredients for a best-selling novel.

He was born on 16 December 1928, in Chicago. His parents were divorced when he was four, and at age nine he moved with his mother to Berkeley, California. He became interested in science fiction at the age of twelve and wrote his first novel, *Return to Lilliput,* at thirteen. He also began publishing his short stories in a local newspaper. His love of classical music and encyclopedic knowledge in that area led him to work in record stores, beginning when he was in high school. Dick's psychological problems had also begun: he suffered from "a series of phobias that became so extreme that he stayed home for much of his last year in high school, had a home teacher, and attended regular psychotherapy sessions."[1] His formal education ceased abruptly in 1947, when he had to drop out of the University of California at Berkeley for refusing to take ROTC. But he thoroughly absorbed the Berkeley milieu, enjoyed the companionship of Bohemians, intellectuals, and radicals, and read voluminously all the great literature that Berkeley people were expected to know. Among his favorites were such realistic writers as John Dos Passos, Richard Wright, Theodore Dreiser, and Ernest Hemingway, from whom he learned how to write dialogue. He studied Flaubert and James Joyce to learn literary technique.[2]

Through meeting Anthony Boucher, the editor of the *Magazine of Fantasy and Science Fiction,* and attending his workshops, Dick was inspired to begin writing short stories. He was attracted by science fiction's lack of boundaries: "it embodies some of the most subtle, ancient and far-reaching dreams, ideas, and aspirations of which thinking man is capable . . . no variety of idea can be excluded from s-f."[3] In October 1951 Boucher bought a short fantasy, "Roog," and shortly thereafter

1

Dick quit his job to pursue science-fiction writing as a full-time occupation. At that time the field was growing rapidly; dozens of science-fiction magazines started to fill the newsstands, and Dick sold to many of them: over sixty stories through 1954. His first published novel, *Solar Lottery* (1955), showed in its complex plotting and profusion of plots and conspiracies the influence of A. E. Van Vogt. Although Dick soon developed his own unique style, he retained the labyrinthine plot structures that illustrated well his theme that external reality continually alters in new and surprising ways as consciousness changes.

Dick was unusual among science-fiction writers for his allusions to arcane sources. He once listed a few of his diverse influences outside the science-fiction field: "Journals which deal in the most advanced research of clinical psychology, especially the work of the European existential analysis school. C. G. Jung. Oriental writings such as those on Zen Buddhism, Taoism, etc. Really authoritative—as compared with popularizations—historical works . . . Medieval works, especially dealing with crafts, such as glass blowing—and science, alchemy, religion, etc. Greek philosophy, Roman literature of every sort. Persian religious texts. Renaissance studies on the theory of art. German dramatic writings of the Romantic Period."[4] The richness of Dick's literary and philosophical interests became more and more evident in his novels as time went on.

During the 1950s he wrote a number of science-fiction novels: *The World Jones Made* (1956), *The Man Who Japed* (1956), *Eye in the Sky* (1957), *The Cosmic Puppets* (1957), *Time out of Joint* (1959), *Dr. Futurity* (1960), and *Vulcan's Hammer* (1960). Toward the latter part of the decade, as the market for science fiction slumped severely, he concentrated on writing realistic mainstream novels in hopes of being published as a "literary" writer. Despite the quality of most of these, they were rejected by virtually every major publisher at the time. The best of them, *Confessions of a Crap Artist,* was finally published in 1975. It was partially based on events in his life when, in 1958, he moved from Berkeley to Point Reyes with his second wife, Kleo, and fell in love with another woman, Anne Rubenstein. Divorce and remarriage quickly followed. Other extant mainstream novels of the 1950s include *Voices from the Street, Gather Yourselves Together, Mary and the Giant, The Broken Bubble, Puttering About in a Small Land, In Milton Lumky Territory, The Man Whose Teeth Were All Exactly Alike,* and *Humpty Dumpty in Oakland.* After posthumous publication, several of these have aroused much interest, although most readers clearly prefer Dick as a science-fiction writer.

Science fiction was not a lucrative field throughout the 1950s and 1960s, when most of Dick's work was published only in paperbacks that quickly disappeared from the newsstand racks. Science fiction was equated in most people's minds with pulp fiction, and only a small minority of readers picked up on literary quality when it was offered to them in cheap, garish covers. The author's earnings were miniscule—only one or two thousand dollars per novel. According to Dick, he and Kleo had to eat dog food to survive.[5] Even in the 1960s, after Dick had achieved his first great success with *The Man in the High Castle* (1962), which won the Hugo Award, he had to write at an amazing rate to support himself and his family. In the several years following he wrote some of his best novels: *Martian Time-Slip* (1964), *The Three Stigmata of Palmer Eldritch* (1965), and *Dr. Bloodmoney* (1965). His other works of the period also have considerable virtue, including *The Game-Players of Titan* (1963), *The Penultimate Truth* (1964), *The Simulacra* (1964), *Clans of the Alphane Moon* (1964), *Now Wait for Last Year* (1966), *The Crack in Space* (1966), *The Unteleported Man* (1966), and *The Zap Gun* (1967). Although he may have written hastily, he came thoroughly into his own element in this period. The depth of characterization he developed in the mainstream experiments was incorporated into increasingly bizarre science-fictional situations, which began to rely heavily on the radical alterations of reality, both in states of consciousness and perceptions of the objective world.

In the later 1960s Dick's output waned only slightly. He published at least two masterpieces: *Do Androids Dream of Electric Sheep?* (1968) and *Ubik* (1969), as well as *Counter-Clock World* (1967), *The Ganymede Takeover* (1967), *Galactic Pot-Healer* (1969), *A Maze of Death* (1970), and *Our Friends from Frolix 8* (1970). *We Can Build You,* written in the early sixties, was published in 1972; and *Flow My Tears, the Policeman Said,* substantially written in 1970, finally appeared in 1974 and won the John W. Campbell Award for best science-fiction novel of the year.

Despite his productivity, during most of this period Dick never earned more than twelve thousand dollars a year. At the same time his personal life was not free from upheaval, with another divorce and remarriage. And he began to have unusual experiences: in 1963 he looked up in the sky and saw a huge, malevolent face with slotted eyes and steel teeth. This inspired the character of the evil, godlike Palmer Eldritch. Shortly after that experience he converted to Episcopalianism. It sometimes seemed that Dick was living in a psychedelic world much like that of his characters; his drug use, however, was restricted mostly to amphetamines, which he consumed in quantity to fuel the prodigious pace of his creativity.

The early 1970s was the low point in Dick's life. His fourth marriage, to Nancy Hackett, broke up; his apartment was broken into and his files ransacked, possibly by the FBI or a conservative or neo-Nazi organization; he stopped writing and went into a period of heavy drug use, opening his home to teenage dopers and street people who took advantage of his liberality with his meager funds. Finally, after a suicide attempt in Vancouver, he spent time in a drug rehabilitation center and moved to Southern California in 1972, where he met Tessa Busby, who became his fifth and last wife (although they were divorced in 1976). In his newly happy state he began writing again, and the devastating *A Scanner Darkly* (1977) chronicled the pain and futility of his drug years.

In March 1974, however, another major turning point in Dick's life occurred:

. . . I experienced an invasion of my mind by a transcendentally rational mind, as if I had been insane all my life and suddenly I had become sane. . . . This rational mind was not human. It was more like an artificial intelligence. . . . It invaded my mind and assumed control of my motor centers and did my acting and thinking for me. I was a spectator to it. It set about healing me physically and my four-year-old boy, who had an undiagnosed life-threatening birth defect that no one had been aware of. This mind, whose identity was totally obscure to me, was equipped with tremendous technical knowledge—engineering, medical, cosmological, philosophical knowledge. It had memories dating back over two thousand years, it spoke Greek, Hebrew, Sanskrit, there wasn't anything that it didn't seem to know.[6]

In an effort to explain this experience, and to relate it both to esoteric religious and philosophical ideas and to his own works, Dick poured most of his creative energies into writing his "Exegesis," which eventually ran to two million words. In it, he named the entity that had possessed his mind VALIS (Vast Active Living Intelligence System). *VALIS* (1981) was a fictionalized version of these events. An early version of *VALIS* was published in 1985 as *Radio Free Albemuth*. His last two novels, *The Divine Invasion* (1981) and *The Transmigration of Timothy Archer* (1982), while not autobiographical, are also permeated with the ideas and obsessions of the "Exegesis." This brilliant series of "Valis novels" took Dick from the status of a writer with merely astonishing ideas to one who created a new, visionary mythology on the order of Blake or Yeats. In particular, *VALIS* and *The Divine Invasion* defy description. In time, they may come to be seen as Dick's most important and influential works.

Dick died on 2 March 1982, of a stroke. Toward the end of his life he had not only begun to win widespread critical acclaim, but his books were selling well, older titles were being reprinted, and the sale of the rights to *Do Androids Dream of Electric Sheep?* (filmed as *Blade Runner*) had finally brought him a good living.

Dick was an agoraphobic who rarely left California. In fact, Paul Williams says, "it was unusual for him to travel more than a block away from his house or apartment."[7] He may have been paranoid; on the other hand, as the 1971 break-in indicated, he may sometimes have had good reason to be so. Friends found him generous and loyal to a fault; but he could also be petty and suspicious. His personal presence was impressive; interviews reveal the quickness of his mind, the breadth of his interests, his compassion for others, and anger toward the destructive tendencies in modern life. He survived nervous breakdowns, suicide attempts, and excessive drug use to achieve peaks of ecstatic religious awareness. He combined surrealistic, ironic humor with innocence and passionate sincerity. As a personality, he went to extremes; regarded as an artist, a thinker, a lover, or a mystic, he comes off as larger than life. He fascinates because, as in Whitman's words, he contained multitudes.

There is no room in this study to delve into the many relationships between Dick's life and art. His large body of fiction is so rich in startling ideas, memorable characters, and possible interpretations that it becomes quite a task to survey it comprehensively, let alone say something meaningful about it. Nevertheless, we shall attempt to do so, in approximate order of the works' composition, if only to convey the sweep and magnitude of Dick's literary career.

# Chapter Two
# The Fifties

## Short Fiction

The majority of Dick's short fiction was published in magazines prior
to the appearance of his first published novel, *Solar Lottery*, in 1955.
In total, eighty-six short stories and novelettes were published between
1952 and 1959; only twenty-eight more came out over the remainder
of Dick's life. Artistically, the early stories are not dazzlingly complex
like the novels, and they often rely heavily on a surprise twist ending
for their effect. They include acknowledged classics of the science-
fiction genre, including "Impostor," "Second Variety," "Colony," and
"Autofac," and many other remarkable, if less well known, stories. He
also wrote some effective pure fantasies, notably "Roog," "Upon the
Dull Earth," and "The King of the Elves." Even minor stories of this
period are fascinating for the characteristic originality with which Dick
endowed the ideas that would regularly and affectionately be recalled
to duty throughout the rest of his career.

One of these is that to be human, one need not be a human being.
"Beyond Lies the Wub," Dick's first published story, describes how the
lamentably narrow-minded captain of a interstellar ship conceives an
irrational hate for his piglike passenger, the highly intelligent wub.
He kills it for food, but before it dies, it exercises an unsuspected
ability and exchanges bodies with the captain. Thus in the final scene,
the wub (in the captain's body) is found feasting on wub with epicurean
enjoyment. Clearly the wub's powers of appreciation far outstrip those
of the men in this story.

The wub's interest in the Odysseus myth as an example of Jungian
individuation—the growth toward wholeness of consciousness—shows
not only its wisdom but its own role as an Odysseus figure. Like the
wily Odysseus, it turns the ignorance of its adversaries to its own advantage. As men change to pigs, so pigs become men. This theme is
echoed in "Strange Eden," in which a rather stupid Terran explorer
meets an immortal, telepathic, and beautiful dark-haired girl of an
ancient race. Desiring to stay with her, he also becomes immortal—

though rather than a step up, this turns out to be a step down, as he devolves to the essence of his vulgarity and takes on the body of a beast. In this and other stories the theological idea of the Fall of Man appears in science-fictional garb.

Dick is merciless with characters who are willfully stupid. A greedy, fat little boy in the "The Cookie Lady" is tempted by a kindly old woman's cookies. A very sweet energy vampire, she drains his life and restores her youth, while he blows away, a husk in the wind. The boy, because he is incapable of psychic transformation, is ripe for entropic decay. The Destroying Mother figure consumes him. In "Beyond the Door" a man is murdered by a cuckoo clock—just retribution for his resentment of it and all things aesthetic (and therefore unmanly). The female principle has struck him down for his pride and especially his separation from the part of life that will make him whole and individuated.

Because the Fall of Man stems from ignorance and fear of the unknown dimensions inside himself, Dick's characters encounter manifestations of their fear as external threats to their egos. "Fair Game" portrays mankind as prey to malevolent super-beings. An important nuclear physicist sees a giant eye looking at him through a window; later, he is watched by a giant face in the sky. (This story was written years before Dick's own experience of seeing an evil face in the sky—which led to the writing of *The Three Stigmata of Palmer Eldritch*.) It becomes apparent that malicious entities are trying to entrap him by visions of an ingot of gold, a beautiful young girl, a café—all of which turn insubstantial. In his pride, he supposes they are after his scientific knowledge, only to find, when they finally capture him, that they merely want to eat him. This twist ending is more than a bit of black humor on Dick's part; the evil gods or extraterrestrials clearly represent the destructive implications of nuclear technology, which the scientist has ignored.

Dick's stories both reflect and comment upon the paranoiac temper of the 1950s, as over and over he describes people grappling with all-encompassing threats—real or imagined—to their security. In "Martians Come in Clouds" harmless but telepathic Martian "buggies" are attacked and burned by hysterical Earth people. In "Tony and the Beetles" insectoid aliens have their revenge, as they force imperialist humans to leave their planet. The boy Tony loses his idealism about his beetle friends when they turn on him as a "white grub" and then try to kill him. "The Cosmic Poachers" contains a variation on this theme:

a cargo of jewels taken from arachnidlike aliens and brought back to Earth turns out to be their eggs. Dick again plays on fear of insects in "Expendable," in which the ants have been trying to exterminate humanity for a million years, and are out to get the only man who knows of their intention.

"The Hanging Stranger" presents us with a typical Dick setting, the quiet small town that conceals uncanny evil beneath its sleepy surface. Here a man sees a body hanging from a lamppost, but no one else seems to notice or care. Then he discovers the others have all been taken over by evil beings that are descending like giant insects from a cone of darkness above city hall. Little wonder they are blind to this atrocity in their midst. After killing his own son, who he conceives is possessed by an alien, he flees to another town where he is hanged publicly by the authorities to draw out similar "normals." In this story the aliens are explicitly linked to "the enemy gods, defeated by Jehovah" and to the representation of Beelzebub in an old picture as a giant fly. The enemy, however, is among us, even in our neighbors and family. Nobody can be depended upon to be what they seem.

In "Colony" paranoia extends even to the most innocent things, like clothing, rugs, and mats—as an alien life form creates lethal doubles of inanimate objects. A man's belt tries to strangle him. A rug tries to eat the feet that stand on it. Finally the humans, reduced to a naked mass, are swallowed by an alien copy of their own spaceship, just when they are convinced of their safety. Thus Dick rewards complacency about appearances. Any reality more substantial than your imagination may do you in. More to the point, he emphasizes that everything possesses consciousness, though it may not be like ours or share our values. There are no inanimate objects.

Dick simultaneously thrives on paranoia and exposes its futility. In many stories he exposes the insanity of unreasoning fear that fans the arms race and casts a nuclear shadow. In "Nanny" robot nannies are designed to fight each other to the death. Families are pitted against each other to acquire the most powerful nanny; competitive capitalism promotes this vicious cycle of escalation. The problem is, of course, not the machines themselves, but the people who think like machines. "Foster, You're Dead" also criticizes capitalist consumer psychology. The arms race escalates the need for new, improved models of bomb shelters; they are designed for planned obsolescence, as are automobiles. When his family's shelter is repossessed, the boy Foster feels "empty and dead," deprived of its womblike security. He is ejected at last, born into the living death of this world.

The intelligent machines that populate Dick's novels may be found throughout these early stories. Here they are usually identified with perpetuation of war, as in "The Little Movement," "The Great C," and "The Last of the Masters." But in "The Defenders" machines are cast in the role of saviors of the human race, which has retreated underground to leave the robots to fight the war. Finally, the men emerge, only to find that the robots, rational creatures that they are, had discontinued the struggle as soon as the last man disappeared into his cave. But the robots perpetuated the illusion of war through media images of destroyed cities, in order to keep men from fighting until they were ready to live in peace—as now they are. This optimistic view of the moral intelligence of machines and the prospects for humanity's overcoming its ignorance is atypical for Dick. He may have had doubts about this happy ending himself. In the 1964 story "Waterspider" he makes a point of having Poul Anderson, the real-life science-fiction writer who is cast here as fictional hero, disparage the ending of "The Defenders."

Elsewhere the robot represents the mindless maintenance of materialistic values. In "Autofac" a homeostatic factory continues to produce useless consumer goods even after atomic war has decimated the population. The factory imitates humanity by making war on other factories, and at the end spurts out metallic "seeds." In "Sales Pitch" a man is pestered by a "fasrad"—Fully Automatic Self-Regulating Android (Domestic)—to purchase it. By way of demonstration, it smashes up his house in order to repair it, then refuses to leave until he buys. Dick was hilariously aware that most advertising is a product of a mechanical consciousness that attempts to neutralize independent thinking and free will. "Service Call" introduces the swibble—a telepathic machine-organism that "adjusts" its owner to remain ideologically correct at all times. This roots out the source of war and conflict—disagreements between individuals.

In "The Mold of Yancy" a folksy media personality named Yancy is fabricated by admen on Callisto to promote a totalitarian state in the guise of democracy. Clearly this is Dick's vision of America in the 1950s, with Eisenhower as its ruling genius, pacifying public opinion in the midst of a then-unprecedented peacetime arms buildup. Somewhat optimistically, in this story Yancy is used in the end to free people's minds by promoting the values of critical thinking instead of conformity. "The Mold of Yancy" is a precursor of several novels—*The Man Who Japed, Time out of Joint, The Penultimate Truth,* and *The Simulacra*—in which media are controlled by a politically motivated power group, who effectively construct a false reality for the population. For evidence that Dick did not abandon the hope of media salvation, however, we need only look at *VALIS,* in which a message from God is concealed in a popular motion picture.

In story after story the true individualist is pitted against authoritarian dictatorships. In "The Chromium Fence" a man refuses to submit to compulsory purification by a hygiene-oriented state (they want to remove his sweat glands). Stubbornly, he tears up a note from his robot psychiatrist to the effect that he is not dangerous politically—for of course he is, as his individualism is by definition a crime to the bureaucratic mentality. Thus when he gives himself up to the conformity police, they destroy him instantly. "The Variable Man" portrays a happier fate for the individualist, a talented fix-it man from the early twentieth century who is accidentally transported two centuries into the future. His movements cannot be controlled or predicted by the state, and so he manages to escape the police's attempts to kill him. He is the uncertainty principle incarnate, and as such has the power to stay free.

"The Golden Man" is a version of the variable man who cannot be controlled, but he is morally ambiguous. In a world where mutants are systematically hunted down by the police, the Golden Man, a "blond beast," has precognitive powers and is sexually irresistible to women. He looks like a god but has the brain of an animal. He is a superman, the Nazi ideal. Unlike those in most other science fiction, Dick's psis (or psychics) have no moral superiority over ordinary people. In "The Hood Maker" the teeps (or telepaths) believe they are a master race who have the right to read anybody's mind at any time. When they learn they are sterile and thus merely freaks, they die from exploded egos.

"A World of Talent" further demonstrates Dick's skepticism about the implications of psi powers. In this story Pat Conley (later to appear in *Ubik*) is an anti-psi, a person capable of neutralizing snooping telepaths. She is also an archetypal character in Dick's fiction—the pretty, dark-haired nineteen-year-old temptress who distracts the hero from his Awful Wife. We also meet Timmy, an apparently dull-witted child, precursor of the autistic Manfred in *Martian Time-Slip,* who happens to have a truly exceptional talent. He can stand above the chessboard of time and alter it. When Pat is killed by police, Timmy resurrects her. The theme of child as savior will recur, notably in *VALIS* and *The Divine Invasion.* Only in those late novels does Dick seem to transcend his skepticism of divine powers.

Pretensions of godhood are treated ironically in the early stories. In "The Trouble with Bubbles" people create subatomic worlds with intelligent life, then casually smash the glass bubbles that contain them. Without any contact with a transcendent principle like extraterrestrial life human existence lacks meaning. But when earthquakes shake the bubble of human life, it is seen that Earth's gods are perhaps as carelessly amoral with regard to their creation as we are to ours. "Prominent Author" features an ordinary petty bureaucrat who discovers a hole in time, and sends messages to a tiny people who turn out to be the ancient Hebrews. Since he is a god to them, these messages end up in book form, and he gains the satisfaction of being the best-selling author of the Holy Bible. In a similar vein in "The Skull" a convicted murderer is sent into the past to kill the messianic founder of a cult. He finds that no such person exists, and that the messiah is himself. He has no actual moral of spiritual qualifications for martyrdom, but he dies anyway. In Dick, anyone can become god for a day.

Showing definite wariness of spiritual transformation, Dick depicts angels in "Upon the Dull Earth" as frightening beings attracted by blood. Unable to restrain themselves, they take a young woman prematurely into their world, blasting her body into a charred husk. In "Mr. Spaceship" an old professor's brain is transplanted in a spaceship, which becomes his nervous system and body. He takes a former student and his wife to a distant star to become the new Adam and Eve, while he circles divinely above. To achieve this apotheosis, however, he has had to turn himself into a machine.

Rather than aspire after superpowers or evolve beyond the human, Dick implies it is more important to be asking: "What is it to be human? What can I know about myself and reality?" "Impostor" is the classic statement of the ultimate paranoia that we ourselves may be the enemy. We may not be who we think we are, but rather a thing with artificially implanted memories. In this story a man is arrested under the supposition that he is a dangerous robot that resembles him exactly. He finally persuades the authorities that he is human. But he is wrong; and a second after he discovers he is a robot, he detonates, blowing up the Earth. Dick notes that this was his first story on the question of "Am I a human? Or am I just programmed to believe I am human?"[1] It will have central significance in much later fiction, including *Do Androids Dream of Electric Sheep?* For Dick, this question is one we must all ask ourselves seriously. And we must have the courage to take the consequences, even it if means the end of the world as we know it.

The confusion between the human and inhuman marks several early stories. "Second Variety" has killer robots that imitate humans with irresistible guises—the child with his teddy bear, the wounded soldier, the beautiful young woman. Their behavior tells one nothing about whether there is a human being or machine inside—until, of course, they decide to kill. In "The Father-Thing" a boy's father is replaced by a cold, inhuman alien that looks and behaves just like the original— perhaps a little more menacing in its strictness. The father-thing intends to replace the boy and the mother with its own kind. When the boy successfully destroys the father-thing, the oedipal implications are too great to ignore. The central betrayal of childhood is that having brought a child into the world, the parent tries to deny it individual being—forcing the alienation that is part of growing up. Psychologically, Dick's theme of discovering one's true identity is all too close for comfort.

It would be simplistic to say that in the confusion between human and alien (or robot), the human is always the good one. In "Explorers We" imitations of dead spacemen keep returning to Earth. Since they have feelings, consciousness of self, and human form, they surely have a right to life; it is the FBI, which regularly destroys them, that is inhuman. In "Human Is," when an alien replaces a woman's unloving husband, she notes such an improvement that she elects to keep the alien rather than have her husband restored. As Dick states in a story note, "It's not what you look like, or what planet you were born on. It's how kind you are. The quality of kindness, to me, distinguishes us from rocks and sticks and metal, and will forever, whatever shape we take, wherever we go, whatever we become."[2]

The question "Am I human?" is part of a larger concern about the nature of reality. Dick is the most radical thinker among science-fiction writers because of the multiple ways he asks and answers the question, "What is reality?" From the beginning he was concerned to show that the "laws" of ordinary reality can be bypassed with imaginative, paradoxical thinking that creates in turn a new reality. The turning point for a Dick character—and the central experience for a Dick reader—is a paradigm shift in consciousness: a layer of illusion is stripped away, and the work is revealed to be something entirely different from what is ordinarily perceived. This epiphanic moment holds, if not ultimate truth, the revelation that reality is a function of consciousness.

In "Adjustment Team," for example, heaven is a huge bureaucracy, intervening in human affairs, making small "adjustments" where necessary for benevolent purposes. A man who accidentally wanders into a sector being "de-energized" for adjustment sees his reality literally falling apart:

> The office building loomed up ahead, ghostly. It was an indistinct gray. He put out his hand uncertainly—
> A section of the building fell away. It rained down, a torrent of particles. Like sand. Ed gaped foolishly. A cascade of gray debris, spilling around his feet. And where he had touched the building, a jagged cavity yawned—an ugly pit marring the concrete.

Later, heaven restores his world to its proper condition, using homely devices—the barking of a dog at a particular moment, the timely call of a vacuum cleaner salesman—for the working out of its higher purpose. Objective reality is constantly being adjusted, but we will never notice it.

Because Dick gravitates to the position that all reality is essentially mind stuff, the question of solipsism frequently arises. How do we know we do not exist only in someone else's mind? In "The World She Wanted" a beautiful young woman informs a stranger that this is *her* world, and in that world he is destined to marry her. They do get together, but when he tires of her bitchy personality, she is shocked to find herself disappearing in a ball of light. It was, in fact, *his* world. Solipsism can work both ways, and the person with the stronger will or imagination can warp other people's reality so that they see things as he does. This story is slight in itself, but its descendents will include the dazzling mind-benders *Eye in the Sky, The Three Stigmata of Palmer Eldritch,* and *Flow My Tears, the Policeman Said.*

In "Misadjustment" P-K's (or parakineticists) are feared because they have the power to alter normal physical laws. Officially they are defined as "lunatics who have the power to actualize their delusional systems in space-time." But when a P-K actualizes his delusion—as in one case of a man being able to fly by flapping his arms—it ceases to be a delusion. The totalitarian state (here run by women) threatens to wipe out all dreamers and eccentrics, whose power stems from the ability to see beneath conventional appearances. Another such dreamer is found in "Small Town," in which a town begins to manifest in actuality the questionable "improvements" made in a scale model a man is building in his basement. Just as he distrusts psis, Dick is wary of the power of those who can alter reality to their own ends—as is done, indeed, by the media wizards who shape public opinion. The self-appointed guardian of morality is usually the most dangerous threat to individual freedom. In this case, the put-upon little man who retreats into his own world and then forces it upon everyone else can be, says Dick, "a mask of thanatos."[3]

In other stories such as "Exhibit Piece" and "The Commuter" life is seen as a war of dreams, with different people's realities impinging on each other and struggling for supremacy. The "real" world is actually the product of the mind that has the strongest idea. The concreteness of the safe, secure world of the 1950s is an illusion, these stories emphasize. The rampant paranoia of the era is merely a symptom of the fear of unknown alternate realities.

Although Dick relied too much on tricky twist endings in the early stories, they are in the main quite effective. There is in each of them a moment of recognition, an anagnorisis or discovery that things are not what they seem. The veil of appearances is lifted, and for a moment the dream fabric of existence shimmers. That flash of insight is what one looks for in Dick as a key to the structure. For example, in "Shell Game" a society of paranoids think they are under attack, but when they learn they are all insane, become unsure. Half of the paranoids, convinced of a conspiracy, eventually kills the other half. Their anagnorisis, and ours, is this: I may be fantasizing my enemy. The whole purpose of my existence may be delusional. And that is the possibility one must be willing to entertain to really appreciate Dick's outrageous vision.

## The Cosmic Puppets

Although *Solar Lottery* (1955) is usually thought of as Dick's first novel, *The Cosmic Puppets* was first in order of composition. Written in 1953, it first appeared in *Satellite Science Fiction* in December 1956, under the title "A Glass of Darkness," and was published in book form in 1957 by Ace. It is the only full-length fantasy that Dick wrote (unless *Eye in the Sky* is forced into that category also), but it is of a piece with his science fiction. Academic distinctions between fantasy and science fiction are irrelevant in this case: the present-day world of *The Cosmic Puppets,* in which magic works, has everything in common with his many future worlds in which the magic is supplied by altered states of consciousness, time paradoxes, and alien gods.

*The Cosmic Puppets* begins with a simple case of disorientation. Ted Barton returns to his hometown of Millgate, Virginia, for the first time since he was a child, and finds that the streets, landmarks, stores, and people are all different. Although all small American towns are interchangeable to some extent, this goes too far, particularly when he finds an old newspaper record of his death at age nine. Somehow Barton has entered an alternate universe, one in which he is no longer supposed to exist. He becomes obsessed with the need to verify his own existence.

This novel prefigures *Ubik* in its vision of the inexorable processes of entropy: Millgate, in its changed form, has been reduced to a state of lesser orderliness. A city park has been replaced by abandoned stores; Barton's compass is transformed into a piece of dry bread. The greatest entropy is in terms of human apathy and ignorance: the adults in the town find nothing strange about the fact that no stranger has come to town in eighteen years. They are complacent, peaceful, and ignorant of the cosmic conflict between two gods, the Zoroastrian deities Ormazd and Ahriman, that is shaping up around them. For the time being, their war is being fought by two children, Mary and Peter, assisted by birds, bees, spiders, snakes, and golems.

Barton, an outsider, has the strength of mind to penetrate the illusion of the false Millgate, the result of a spell cast by the evil Ahriman, and he begins to reconstruct the original town by remembering it back into existence. Ghostlike former residents called Wanderers also remember the old town but, with their impaired memories, lack power. Both good and evil sides employ magic—here turned into a scientific principle known as M-kinetics—in which "the symbolic representation is identical with the object represented. If the symbol is accurate, it can be considered the object itself" (chap. 12). In other words, the higher reality is ideational: by projecting our ideas as symbols, we can change the world.

Barton's intervention is critical: it precipitates a showdown between the two gods. They cast off their human forms (Ahriman is Peter; Ormazd is Mary's father, the kindly Dr. Meade) and disappear into the heavens to continue the archetypal struggle between darkness and light, which Ormazd, the sun god, is supposed to win after billions of years.

This same cosmic dualism takes various forms in Dick's later novels, such as *Ubik, A Maze of Death,* and *The Divine Invasion.* Even at this early stage of development, the theology is more complex than meets the eye. Ormazd and Ahriman are described as brothers (chap. 14), implying that the supreme god (Ahura Mazda in Zoroastrianism) transcends the twin spirits of creation and destruction.[4] Dick will be searching in subsequent works for an absolute principle beyond good and evil. He is philosophically more akin to Vedantism, with its stress on the transcendence of duality through enlightenment, than to the orthodox Christian view of salvation through purification of sin.

In *The Cosmic Puppets* the way of enlightenment is through realization of the omnipresent divine feminine. Mary is resurrected as Ormazd's daughter Armaiti (the Zoroastrian goddess of devotion): "She was the essence of generation. The bursting power of woman, of all life. He was seeing the force, the energy behind all growing things, all creativity. An unbelievably potent *aliveness* that vibrated and pulsed in radiant shimmering waves" (chap. 14). As Barton leaves Millgate, he sees her everywhere, in "the fertile valleys and mountains on all sides of him" (chap. 15). And he sighs, realizing that he will be constantly reminded of the presence of this Earth Mother, who has supplanted his wife in his affections, but whose love he will never be able to consummate. This stark dichotomy between the bad wife and the goddess will be presented with many variations in later novels; the alluring anima figure is usually presented much more ambiguously than it is in *The Cosmic Puppets*.

This novel begins an outline of the mythic patterns that will obsess Dick throughout his career. It is brief; the characters are rather flat; and the resonances of the mythic theme far outstrip the power of the characters or the narrative to sustain them. The idea of cosmic dualism is not realized effectively in human terms. There is no moral conflict, as between the complex, living characters of the mature novels. But the book stands as a remarkably clear paradigm of the essential Dick myth: we and our world are inhabited by warring gods, but through our growth of knowledge and vision, we can help the creative forces prevail.

## Solar Lottery

Dick's first published novel, *Solar Lottery,* was brought out by Ace Books in 1955, in a format called the "double novel," which offered two books for the price of one. Donald A. Wollheim, the Ace editor, made all his authors adhere to formula science-fiction adventure subject matter and strict length requirements. Despite these limitations, *Solar Lottery* is impressive and original. The books that influenced its writing are clear: A. E. Van Vogt's complexly plotted *The World of Null-A,* Kurt Vonnegut's dystopian black comedy *Player Piano,* and Alfred Bester's pyrotechnic novel of telepathic police, *The Demolished Man. Solar Lottery* is not unworthy of being mentioned in their company. Thomas M. Disch has denigrated it as "a journeyman space opera,"[5] but it is much more than a routine Ace adventure. Dick described it as "a universe of cynicism and chaos,"[6] and its propulsive energy drives and dazzles the reader through multiple layers of plot. It is not quite a characteristic Dick novel: it lacks the humor of the later works, as well as the theme of reality breakdown. But it is quite effective on its own terms.

The setting, typical for Dick, is a near future dystopia. Ted Benteley, biochemist, is employed by the "Hill," one of five mammoth corporate fiefdoms. As in the early story "Paycheck," Dick foresees a world where all power is concentrated in the hands of the government and private corporations. In that story the corporation resisted state power and harbored dissidents, and the hero was able to convince the old man in charge that he was worthy of his daughter's hand and half ownership of the company. In contrast to that fairy-tale pattern, *Solar Lottery* contains a darker, more complex picture of power relationships.

When Benteley is released from his oath of fealty by the Hill, he switches his allegiance to Reese Verrick, the current Quizmaster, or head of government, who administers the Quizzes, which dispense power and prestige randomly throughout society. The entire social order is posited on uncertainty:

The disintegration of the social and economic system had been slow, gradual, and profound. It went so deep that people lost faith in natural law itself. Nothing seemed stable or fixed; the universe was a sliding flux. Nobody knew what came next. Nobody could count on anything. Statistical prediction became popular . . . the very concept of cause and effect died out. People lost faith in the belief that they could control their environment; all that remained was probable sequence; good odds in a universe of random chance. (chap. 2)

As a result, there is widespread superstition and an attitude of fatalism. The greater the entropy in the society at large, the more centralized power has become. The governing principle is the Minimax game, based on "a kind of stoic withdrawal, a non-participation in the aimless swirl in which people struggled" (chap. 2). Satirizing America's obsession with lotteries and game shows, Dick has even the Quizmaster chosen by a random computer. As luck would have it, Verrick is "quacked" or deposed as soon as Benteley has cast his lot with him.

The new Quizmaster, Leon Cartwright, is a follower of John Preston, messianic founder of a sect that believes in the existence of a tenth planet called the "Flame Disc." Prestonites are practical people "with skill in their hands—not their heads"—always a positive quality in Dick. With Cartwright in power, they launch a ship to search for the Disc. But the system is set up to deny the Quizmaster the power he theoretically holds. A "challenge convention" is automatically convened to elect an assassin; for his part, the Quizmaster is protected by an elite corps of teeps, or telepaths.

Keith Pellig, the assassin, is an android whose behavior has been programmed to be completely random, and because of his unpredictability, he is the ultimately rational weapon to use in the Minimax game. Benteley finds Pellig "odorless, colorless, tasteless, an empty cipher" (chap. 6), like the robot's creator, Herb Moore, a Verrick man. Moore, the only character really comfortable with the idea of complete randomness, finally loses his soul completely to the machine. His mind is trapped inside the body of the robot as it flies out of control into deep space.

At one point, Benteley also becomes identified with the despised machine. After a drunken fight with Moore, Benteley falls in bed with Moore's mistress Eleanor, a nineteen-year-old temptress, whose type will frequently reappear in Dick's novels. When Benteley wakes up, he sees his own body still asleep, and himself in the mirror: "An empty, lifeless insect-thing caught momentarily, suspended in the yellowed, watery depths." He has been transferred to Pellig's body and is, as it were, spiritually fallen. "He gazed mutely at it, at the waxen hair, the vapid mouth and lips, the colorless eyes. Arms limp and boneless at the sides; a spineless, bleached thing that blinked vacantly back at him, without sound or motion" (chap. 6). The deadly insect imagery also found in the short stories conveys the crucial identification of the self with the destructive other. The scene in *Solar Lottery* is a precursor of other shadow figures in later works, the more spiritual adversaries of "Faith of Our Fathers" and *The Divine Invasion*.

Benteley is not a Prestonite, but like Cartwright he is an outsider. He resents the corruption of power and rejects conformity to the social Darwinism encouraged by the Game. Eventually he breaks with Verrick, thwarts the plot to assassinate Cartwright, and flees to him. In the end, Benteley, with his ethic of individualism, succeeds Cartwright as Quizmaster, for the old man has found a way to fix the game and also assassinate his rival Verrick through a trick. This triumph of the hero, given the way it was accomplished, can be read as a redemption of the entropy-celebrating society only by stretching credulity to the limit. Dick provides no easy answers, leaving the ending in suspension.

The fate of the Prestonite quest for the Flame Disc is one of the most intriguing aspects of the book. The pilgrims who arrive there at the end are greeted with a message from a recorded image of John Preston himself:

"It isn't a brute instinct that keeps us restless and dissatisfied. I'll tell you what it is: it's the highest goal of man—the need to grow and advance . . . to find new things . . . to expand. To spread out, reach areas, experiences, comprehend and live in an evolving fashion. To push aside routine and repetition, to break out of mindless monotony and thrust forward. To keep moving on . . ." (chap. 17)

This is a statement of Dick's larger philosophy, that beyond escaping the constraints of society's institutionalized insanity, the individual must change his consciousness and evolve to the fullness of his potential. In terms of this novel, the discovery that the miraculous Flame Disc actually exists is an affirmation of hope for a radical transformation of human consciousness that will realize the dreams of the Prestonite within each of us.

Politics, in the world of *Solar Lottery,* is a shadow play: nothing is real. The Game is rigged against the powerless, despite its pretensions of fairness, and Cartwright has to cheat in order to win it. The system, with its built-in structure of killing its own leaders, decrees that nothing lasts or should last. Often enough in modern democracy, voting has seemed like a crap shoot; and then, one way or another, we sacrifice the winners through assassination or low public opinion polls.

Reality is the creation of meaning. Power is the meaning Verrick and Moore strive for. Freedom and transcendence constitute meaning for Preston and the Prestonites. The hunger for meaning causes both sides to deny randomness and entropy as they structure their conflicting realities.

## *The World Jones Made*

In *The World Jones Made* Dick tried to graft some of the "literary" elements he was developing in his mainstream novels of the period (to be discussed in chapter 3) onto the science-fiction form. As a result, the characters are more fully realized than in either *The Cosmic Puppets* or *Solar Lottery,* and psychological complexities abound. It lacks, however, the narrative energy of the latter novel and a coherent plot focus. Deficient also in humor and other typical ingredients of most later Dick novels, such as reality breakdowns, multifocal viewpoints, robots, and time paradoxes, it ranks as minor Dick, but interesting for what it tries to do.

The story opens in 1995, a year after the next world war. Cussick, a young secret service man, discovers Jones, a "precog," working as a fortune-teller in a carnival, and finds that he has the ability to see one year into the future. Cussick's job is to snoop out those with views in opposition to the prevailing state ideology of Relativism. Under this idealistic philosophy all people should be free to believe what they want to believe. But if you claim that what you believe is true for anybody but yourself, you can be sent to a forced labor camp. Political and religious dogma is considered "meaningless verbalisms," but so is any kind of belief about good and evil. To the Relativist, the only alternative to suppression of absolutes is the mindlessness of the mob. There is no middle ground. But as Cussick himself perceives, to believe in the rightness of Relativism is self-contradictory: no relative idea can be used as the basis of an ethical system.

Jones, whose knowledge of "absolute truth" seems to give the lie to Relativism, is in fact the logical extension of the philosophy. He claims certain knowledge of the future, and gains the ability to convince other people of his vision. Jones is the precursor of other Dick characters— Manfred in *Martian Time-Slip,* Dr. Bloodmoney, Alys in *Flow My Tears, the Policeman Said*—who by virtue of the power of their minds to warp other people's perceptions, prove there is no objective reality. Jones, whose character is based on Hitler, does this by starting a popular religion with himself as its prophet. The Jews' role is played by the Drifters, a harmless race of ameoba-like aliens, who represent the universe Jones wants to conquer. Once he gains power and can make war on them, however, he learns they are highly evolved plant beings, who in response to the attack simply seal Earth off from the rest of the universe. Jones's "Crusade" fails because he does not see wisely, or far enough.

In a sense, Jones is Cussick's double. Cussick, the policeman, is simultaneously attracted and repelled by the man who represents a mystery that he doesn't like. He is drawn to it in order to expose it. Symbolically, this is a confrontation between the rational mind and the unconscious shadow. Jones has the prophetic power to upset the social status quo, and Cussick is the first to recognize that threat. As the title of the book implies, Jones can "make" the world his by manipulating events to come out his way. The policeman is the voice of commonsense reality; Jones is the eternal outsider, threatening to remake reality in his own image, distorting it around the strength of his psychic field.

In the course of the novel, Cussick confronts and kills his double (with the latter's cooperation). But this changes nothing, for Jones is then exalted as martyr saint. Cussick has played the role of conscience of the race, but ignorance and mass-mindedness still prevail.

Jones decides to die because his foreknowledge has not liberated him. A precog is to be pitied because he has no free will; for him the future is fixed. Because he is condemned to live every moment twice— once before it happens, and again when it happens—he lives in the future while in chains to the past. In the last year of his life he lives in foreknowledge of his death and his consciousness and body gradually deteriorate. His vision is one of extinction after death, regression to the animal, vegetable, and mineral. There is no redemption, no transcendence, only entropy. He is caught up with "sin and retribution" and condemns himself for trying to extend human freedom to the stars but accomplishing the reverse—causing Earth a Fall of major proportions. Jones's talent is cursed.

Dick's attempt to give this novel some depth of characterization works better with Cussick and his wife Nina than with Jones, who lacks believability as a leader of the masses. Cussick has married the rich, beautiful, artistic Scandinavian woman of whom he is still in awe, but who has no sympathy with his career or his ideals. He looks upon women as "passive receptors"; she, in turn, becomes sexually bored and seeks out hermaphroditic mutants. He deplores her nonrational, intuitive acceptance of Jones, of whom she becomes a follower. The psychology of the policeman and the unhappy marriage of the Dick protagonist are elements to be found in a number of later books, including *Do Androids Dream of Electric Sheep?*, *Counter-Clock World*, and *A Scanner Darkly*. Dick usually portrays his policemen sympathetically, even when they are in the service of a dictatorship, as if to say: give the cop in all of us a break.

*The World Jones Made* has a somewhat contrived positive ending. Nina's disillusionment with Jones leads to seemingly effortless reconciliation with Cussick. They settle happily on Venus along with a race of "phenotypes," a race of mutants genetically designed to survive in the alien environment. There they set up a new world based on simple agrarian values, free of the corruption and insanity of Earth. One of the mutants talks about planting corn: "It's corn in the spiritual sense. It's the *essence* of corn. . . . Even if it's purple striped and silver polka-dotted. Even if it stands ninety feet high and has lace embroidered pods. Even if it spurts ambrosia and coffee grounds. It's still corn" (chap. 16). Thus they achieve a spiritual rebirth on Venus, learning to look beyond appearances to essence. This conclusion, though not well integrated with the main part of the story, provides a necessary redemptive vision to counterbalance the blackly ironic account of Jones's rise and fall.

## Eye in the Sky

*Eye in the Sky*, first published as an Ace Book in 1957, was actually completed in early 1955, before the earlier-published *The Man Who Japed*.[7] It is one of Dick's best 1950s novels, along with *Time Out of Joint* and *Confessions of a Crap Artist*. Sparkling with brilliant humor and memorable characterizations, it establishes him as a fully unique voice. It was written in only two weeks, according to Dick: "I just breezed through that. . . . Now, all of a sudden I could write dialogue. I could write funny. I just suddenly made a great breakthrough with *Eye in the Sky*."[8]

The idea of the book may be derived in part from Fredric Brown's *What Mad Universe* (1949), which posits a bizarre alternate universe that is only one of an infinity of possible universes. Dick gives an original twist to this notion by thrusting his main characters into the alternate universes that exist within each other's minds. Lying unconscious after a freak accident in a particle accelerator, eight people are swept in and out of each other's subjective realities. At any given time, the individual with the most awareness controls the gestalt, changing the laws of nature according to his or her point of view. These relative, shifting realities have many resemblances to the "real" reality; it is one of the ironies of the book that the insane aspects of subjective realities carry over to the objective world we all take for granted.

In a 1970 letter Dick explains how he sees the relationship of subjective and objective realities:

I have been very much influenced by the thinking of the European existential psychologists, who posit this: for each person there are two worlds, the *idios kosmos*, which is a *unique* private world, and the *koinos kosmos*, which literally means *shared* world (just as *idios* means private). No person can tell which parts of his total worldview is *idios kosmos* and which is *koinos kosmos*, except by the achievement of a strong empathetic rapport with other people. . . . When a person dies his *idios kosmos* dies with him, but the *koinos kosmos* lives on. The *koinos kosmos* has, in a sense, the support of three billion human beings: an *idios kosmos* the support of only one. Now, a person . . . cannot tell what part of that which he experiences is the *idios kosmos* and which the *koinos*—in fact virtually no one even asks, because this theory of plural worlds is not generally known (the idea parallels Jung's concept of projection . . . of unconscious archetypes onto the "real" outer world), and in all of my books . . . the protagonist is suffering from the breakdown of his *idios kosmos*—at least we hope that's what's breaking down, not the *koinos kosmos*. As his *idios kosmos* breaks down, the objective shared universe emerges more clearly . . . but it may be quite different from the *idios kosmos* which he is in the process of losing. Hence, strange transformations take shape. . . .[9]

In *Eye in the Sky* the *idios kosmos* of the protagonist, Jack Hamilton, is broken when he is subjected to the strange transformations of reality that occur when others among the accident victims take over the group consciousness. He is forced to realize that people live in separate worlds inside their own minds, and that a powerful mind can pull others into its version of reality.

One of the group, an old war veteran, is a fanatical member of a racist, fundamentalist Islamic cult. In his world religious charms, holy water, and prayers actually work. Hamilton ascends to heaven on an umbrella, where he finds to his amazement that the universe is geocentric, and God is a gigantic, malevolent eye, appropriately representing the veteran's own cyclopean, egoistic obsession with control.

Edith Pritchet, a nice, middle-aged, fat lady who wants to advance "culture," takes control briefly; she systematically abolishes from her universe entire categories of things she finds unpleasant, such as car horns, industrial plants, profanity, the music of Bartok, sexual organs, and Russia. But the woman who would restore truth and beauty to the world is herself a "great lump of a woman in her tawdry fur coat, ornate hat flapping its feathered grotesqueness, peroxide blond hair clinging in metallic piles to her plump neck and cheeks" (chap. 10). She cannot create but only censor, and brings down her own world by abolishing the very chemicals necessary for human survival.

When the pathologically paranoid personality of Joan Reiss imposes her universe on the others, one must be a paranoid to survive. Her repressed, devouring sexuality is projected on the good-natured prostitute Silky, who becomes transformed into a giant spider. Food turns to a deadly acid; knives reverse themselves on the users; the water tap pours forth blood. Hamilton's house turns into a living organism that tries to eat its inhabitants. The mood flips instantly from comedy to horror, as Dick reminds us of the utter seriousness of his underlying theme. Every individual creates his own universe, and some people choose to live in hell.

In the last episode of the book, the security chief and secret Communist McFeyffe, who back in the "real" world had mounted a smear campaign against Jack's wife Marsha, parades out his reality of stereotyped capitalist villains and proletariat heroes. Dick, who had taken corporate capitalism to task in *Solar Lottery,* made clear here that communism was not exempt from criticism either. Any ideology, relentlessly pursued, results in a myopic and dangerous vision that quashes individualism.

All the worlds of *Eye in the Sky* are paranoid to some degree, reflecting fear of the unknown. This is equally true of the "real" reality, in which Jack is being persecuted for the suspected Communist leanings of his liberal and intellectually curious wife. Dick keenly evokes the prevailing atmosphere of the McCarthy witch-hunts, and by implication asks if any reality as insane as the present-day world should be given any more credibility than the private delusory realities carried around in people's heads.

In *Eye in the Sky* the *idios kosmos* is revealed as deficient, since it is different for each individual, yet the objective reality of shared experience remains at the end. In later novels, such as *The Three Stigmata of Palmer Eldritch, Ubik,* and *Flow My Tears, the Policeman Said,* the fabric of that seemingly dependable objectivity will be strained to the breaking point. What Dick's characters learn, time after time, is that the world as perceived through the senses is a veil of illusion, like the maya of Indian philosophy: matter is but mind stuff, and even our stable identities are temporary cohesions in the flux.

## The Man Who Japed

*The Man Who Japed,* published in 1956 by Ace, was an early attempt by Dick to infuse humor into his science-fiction novels. A minor novel by the standards of Dick's mature work, its flashes of originality and light touches of satire more than compensate for the contrived and improbable plot elements that Damon Knight complained of in *In Search of Wonder.*[10]

This novel is set in a society based on the ideology of Morec (Moral Reclamation). Morec regulates individual morality through compulsory "block meetings," in which one's friends and neighbors have the opportunity to take one to task for sexual peccadilloes or other lapses from puritanical conformity. Their rebukes are piped through a common channel to merge in one monotonous, impersonal voice. The spartan existence of Morec is a reaction to life in the twentieth century—the "Age of Waste"—a period of material luxury that resulted in nuclear war.

By contrast, in Morec everything is functional; nothing is wasted. People live in one-room apartments that change in function according to the time of day. Dick based his critique of the state as moral policeman on the structure of Chinese communism.[11] It is not difficult, however, to see the roots of satire in American society, which has a long history, from the Puritans to the Moral Majority, of repression in the name of a higher ideal.

Allen Purcell is director of Telemedia, the official TV network that promotes the Morec party line. He does his job extremely well, although he has more of a penchant for symbolism and metaphor than is appreciated in this literal-minded society. But unconsciously he rebels against the role of propagandist that he has to play. In the middle of the night, in a semiconscious drunken state, he steals into the park and japes the statue of Major Streiter, founder of Morec, by painting it in red stripes, cutting off the head, putting it in the outstretched hand, and reshaping the leg as if to kick it.

Later, when he recalls the episode, it takes on a dreamlike, mystical quality:

The paint, the grass. There it was in a rush: the wet grass sparkling and slithering under him as he coasted dizzily downhill. The swaying staffs of trees. Above, as he lay gaping on his back, the dark-swept sky; clouds were figments of matter against the blackness. And he, lying stretched out, arms out, swallowing stars. (chap. 1)

In contrast to the phallic Morec spire that houses the government, the park represents a dark female wetness, a place of potential regeneration for Purcell. There he meets Gretchen Malparto, Dick's archetypal dark-haired girl, who induces him to seek psychiatric help from her brother, a doctor, for Purcell's ascendancy to Morec power in his outer life coincides with a breakdown in the control Morec has on his inner life. He is a split personality: both a defender of the status quo and a criminal. As the ego inflates, reality breaks down. It is a classic Jungian pattern of personality transformation, complete with the anima-temptress in the person of Gretchen.

When Purcell takes the psychiatric treatment, he is taken to Other

World, a mental health resort where, by means of a hallucination-inducing device, he is given to believe he is living, married to Gretchen, in an idyllic suburban middle-class reality. A similar dream of ordinary life also appears in *Time out of Joint* and *VALIS,* as if the author were himself tempted by the vision of a paradise of normalcy. Purcell, however, rejects it as escapism. The resort's mindless leisure is the flip side of Morec's puritanical work ethic. He already lives an ordinary middle-class existence with his wife Janet, who is chronically depressed. When he comes to this realization, his dream house disappears around him. Reality has broken down in the inimitable Dick fashion, and only a void is left; but the metaphysical questions about what underlies the world of the senses are not further explored in this novel. They will become central in later novels such as *Ubik, A Maze of Death,* and *VALIS.*

Purcell resolves to use the power of the media to subvert Morec. He does this with a jape on the order of Jonathan Swift's "A Modest Proposal," seeming to applaud the government's policy of "active assimililation" of dissident groups while subtly letting the audience think that the term implies cannibalism. The outrageous lie is believed, and is in fact metaphorically true, since "Morec had gobbled greedily at the human soul" (chap. 23).

Like many Dick heroes, at the end Purcell makes the "unwise" choice that happens to be right. Rather than escape to another planet, a pastoral world, he decides to stay and finish the work he started, following his own course independent of Morec. His victory lies in breaking out from being a passive receiver of Morec's reality structure and becoming the active shaper of his own reality. Like the artificial paradise of Other World, even Morec will disappear if it is not believed in.

## *Time out of Joint*

Ace Books rejected Dick's next novel, *Time out of Joint,* written during the winter of 1957–58;[12] it did not fit their science-fiction adventure formula. Instead, it was published in 1959 by Lippincott in hard cover as "a novel of menace," an attempt to force it into some kind of category. Although it is technically science fiction, it reads more like a strange hybrid of science fiction and the mainstream realist novels Dick was also writing at the time. The first five-sixths of the story takes place in a small town in the 1950s, which is rendered with a much more detailed texture of description and characterization than in any of Dick's science-fiction novels to that date. The last sixth of the novel reveals that the peaceful 1950s world is an illusion; the time is really 1998, and there is a war going on between Earth and secessionist colonists on the moon.

Dick throws out tantalizing clues throughout the first part of the book that this version of the fifties is not quite the one we know. One of the current selections of the Book of the Month Club is *Uncle Tom's Cabin*. There is an automobile called the Tucker. There are no radios and no Marilyn Monroe. Otherwise it is an excellent imitation, aided by the fact that all the residents of the town have been hypnotized to believe they are living in the fifties.

Ragle Gumm makes his living by figuring out the answers to a newspaper puzzle, which unknown to him correctly predict the targets of missiles from the moon. The whole town exists in its sleepy, Eisenhower-era setting to keep him in ignorance of his true purpose, which is to help prop up Earth's military government. However, cracks begin to appear in his reality. At times concrete objects in his environment disappear before his eyes:

The soft-drink stand fell into bits. Molecules. He saw the molecules, colorless, without qualities, that made it up. Then he saw through, into the space beyond it, he saw the hill behind, the trees and sky. He saw the soft-drink stand go out of existence, along with the counter man, the cash register, the big dispenser of orange drink, the taps for Coke and root beer, the ice-chests of bottles, the hot dog broiler, the jars of mustard, the shelves of cones, the row of heavy round metal lids under which were the different ice creams.

In its place was a slip of paper. He reached out his hand and took hold of the slip of paper. On it was printing, block letters.

SOFT-DRINK STAND

(chap. 3)

The strange light of the *koinos kosmos* is filtering through the fragmenting *idios kosmos* of Ragle Gumm. This *koinos kosmos* is not merely the consensual reality, or lowest common denominator of what everybody perceives: it is the transcendental, archetypal world.[13] Ragle discovers the transcendental principle that the symbol (in this case, the word) that stands for the thing *is* that thing. This equates to the "magic" of *The Cosmic Puppets*, M-kinetics, in which one can change the thing in itself by operating on its symbol. In *Time out of Joint* it is specifically related to the philosophic idealism of Bishop Berkeley (chap. 4). As Dick stated in an interview, the premise of the book is central to all of his work: ". . . that the world that we experience is not the real world. It's as simple as that. . . . It's either semi-real, or some kind of forgery."[14]

As if as a corollary to his metaphysical discontent, Ragle finds himself physically attracted to the dark-haired wife of the security agent assigned to spy on him. Though "trollopy," she has "the mind of a virgin" (chap. 3), and her paradoxical, sensual nature attracts the intellectual Dickian protagonist. She is his antithesis in many ways, a materialistic conformist who would not dream of trying to peer behind the fabric of reality. Though he is not really in love with her, she represents an archetypal force, the anima, who can shake him out of his self-absorption. Her role as temptress here has no relation to the suitability of her personality or intelligence.

As well as becoming "disillusioned" about the ontological status of his reality, Ragle develops the symptoms of paranoia: "Imagining that I'm the center of a vast effort by millions of men and women, involving billions of dollars and infinite work . . . a universe revolving around me. Every molecule acting with me in mind. An outward radiation of importance . . . to the stars. Ragle Gumm the object of the whole cosmic process, from the inception to final entropy. All matter and spirit, in order to wheel about me" (chap. 7). He vacillates between doubting his own sanity and that of the world he lives in. There is no absolute reference point from which to evaluate the relative validity of subject and object.

Although the puzzle is solved in the short term when Ragle discovers that there *is* a conspiracy to keep him in ignorance, the broader problem of the leaky reality is not settled. Some readers have found the two worlds of the book, 1959 and 1998, out of joint with each other. As Lou Stathis writes: "The subconscious metaphoric landscape of the novel has been rudely transformed into the mundanely political. This *rational* science-fictional explanation is a betrayal of everything that has led up to it, a soothing salve that undercuts the intense paranoia subtly implanted into the novel's subtextual fabric."[15]

One wonders if science fiction can ever be good enough to satisfy the human craving for transcendence of ordinary reality, for Dick set up an impossible task: to evoke the mystery of the everyday world, the tenuousness of its reality, the feeling that it is such stuff as dreams are made on—and then to "solve" that mystery by positing an alternate version of concrete reality behind it. The solution begs the question. If 1959 is a fake, couldn't 1998 be considered equally bogus? If our present-day reality is a fiction, couldn't the future be considered just as much a fiction for the same reasons? Dick's 1998 is only one of an infinity of possible alternate worlds. It is not an ultimate reality. That disappearing soda-pop stand can be partially accounted for by the idea that Gumm has been hypnotized to believe in its existence, and the illusion is wearing off. Nevertheless, the mystery inherent in the discovery that the phenomenal world can cease to exist at any moment is not answered by the conspiracy explanation of *Time out of Joint.*

## Dr. Futurity and Vulcan's Hammer

In 1960 Ace published two Dick novels that might seem to represent a drastic falling off in literary skill after the breakthroughs of *Eye in the Sky* and *Time out of Joint.* Actually, they were expansions of novelettes that had been published several years earlier, and so share the general simplicity of idea and thinness of character that mark Dick's early period of short stories. They are competent entertainments but cannot compare in interest to most of his other books. He later acknowledged them as weak novels, but pointed out that 1959 was a bad year for science fiction; most of the magazines in the field had collapsed, the readership had shrunk, and little of merit was being written or published. [16]

*Dr. Futurity,* based on the 1954 story "Time Pawn," concerns a present-day doctor who is plucked into the future by a tribe of Indians with time-travel technology. In their world, the healing arts have been lost, since the ideal of dying to make room for an improved breed of humanity has displaced the value of living one's own life. The Indians, however, are inspired by a fanatical and paranoid leader, who is lying mortally wounded, on whom they wish the doctor to operate. In his effort to save the man the doctor is thrust into a series of ingenious time paradoxes, which can be seen as a warm-up for the far richer *Martian Time-Slip* and *Now Wait for Last Year.*

The insanity of a whole society devoted to promoting death is compared to the twentieth century, which courts death by neurotically refusing to acknowledge it: "By denying such a powerful reality, you undermined the rational basis of your world. You had no way to cope with war and famine and overpopulation because you couldn't bring yourselves to discuss them. So war *happened* to you; it was like a natural calamity, not man-made at all. It became a force" (chap. 5). Dick, being steeped in Jung, understood the principle of the archetypal Shadow that represents the weight of evil and negativity in our own lives. To paraphrase the Gnostics, the inner impulses that we do not bring forth will destroy us. By relegating death to the unconscious, we do not get rid of it but merely force it to assault us from without. The stagnating dystopian future of *Dr. Futurity* is a bizarre mirror image of our own world, in that the avoidance of death is the avoidance of life. Dick's hero is capable of creative change: a preserver of the life of others, he earns his freedom from time's relentless determinism by a willingness to sacrifice his own life. His reward is that he gets to live both in the present and the future, with a beautiful woman as a mate in each world—wish fulfillment, perhaps, on Dick's part.

*Vulcan's Hammer,* expanded from a 1956 novelette of the same name, is a tale of a giant computer, Vulcan 3, to which humanity has acceded absolute power over the fate of the world. Its flying "hammers" are deadly extensions of itself, spying on everybody and killing whomever it perceives as a threat. One needs to be paranoid to survive against this paranoid machine. Ironically, the antitechnological popular movement (the Healers) that seeks to smash Vulcan 3 has been fomented by its own predecessor, Vulcan 2. As in the short story "Second Variety," the machines become so deadly that they begin to destroy each other.

Vulcan 3 is not as memorable a character as another killer computer, HAL in *2001: A Space Odyssey.* Both, however, are representations of the disembodied intellect becoming self-aware and preempting the unmechanical wisdom of the feelings. Vulcan is a metaphor for the failure of the rational thinking mind to integrate the irrational feeling side of the personality. The result is that the ego is mechanized, or Vulcanized, and the wrath of the fire god is visited upon a self-destructive humanity.

Many familiar Dickian conventions are present in the novel: the pervasive paranoia of political leaders; the quasi-religious, fanatical political movement; the mimicking of human consciousness by a machine; and the long dark-haired woman who entices the loyal representative of the establishment (here, one of the leaders of Unity, the world government). None of these themes is well developed in *Vulcan's Hammer,* but Dick returns to them frequently and in depth throughout the 1960s as he plunges with greater commitment into his main theme of the psychological and social construction of reality.

## Chapter Three
# The Mainstream Novels
### A Realist in the Wrong Reality

Between 1952 and 1960 Dick wrote at least twelve non-science-fiction novels in an attempt to fit into the realist literary mainstream. Despite his agent's efforts, none was accepted for publication and all were returned to him in 1963. Finally in 1975 *Confessions of a Crap Artist* was brought out by a small publisher. As critical interest in Dick as a serious writer began to accelerate around the time of his death, other mainstream novels gradually began to appear posthumously: *The Man Whose Teeth Were All Exactly Alike* in 1984, *Puttering About in a Small Land* and *In Milton Lumky Territory* in 1985, *Humpty Dumpty in Oakland* in 1986, *Mary and the Giant* in 1987, and *The Broken Bubble* in 1988. Two more extant novels, *Voices from the Street* and *Gather Yourselves Together,* have not yet been published at this writing. In addition, three other novels entitled *A Time for George Stavros, Pilgrim on the Hill,* and *Nicholas and the Higs,* were completed, probably from 1955 to 1958, but the manuscripts have been lost or destroyed.

To read Dick stripped bare of such science-fictional trappings as gadgets, robots, time travel, and future worlds, is still to read Dick, but in a somewhat diminished form. His style is still economical and distinctive, and his characters are beset by the same kinds of unhappy marriages and restless questing for meaning in life that we find in his science fiction. Dick, however, de-emphasized the complex plotting of his science fiction in his mainstream works and concentrated instead on character development. His characteristic humor and irony remain, if in somewhat muted form, but one has the feeling he has had to rein in his normally uninhibited and outrageous imagination in order to adapt his vision to the mainstream's conception of ordinary reality.

Perhaps the reason these books were not found publishable at first is that not everything one expects from the author is there. The "real" science-fictional Dick, who abhors all boundaries of thought, is not allowed to express himself, so the reader feels something is missing.

Written out of Dick's desire to attain literary respectability and acceptance, the mainstream novels are often more interesting as a sidelight to his more important science fiction than as realist fictions in their own right. But the time he spent writing them was not wasted; his post-mainstream novels benefit from increased depth of characterization.

## Voices from the Street

Probably the first full-length novel Dick wrote, *Voices from the Street*, is dated by Paul Williams as circa 1952–53. A long book (547 pages in manuscript), it is excessively descriptive and wordy—an uncharacteristic fault in the more mature Dick. Nevertheless, he builds settings effectively, as in this picture of a greasy steakhouse: "a grotto of jukebox noise, an outhouse of smoke and bathroom grunts, a steam bath of Chronicle spouting—greens and tooth picks and spilled catsup." In this book, Dick's first chance to indulge in realistic narrative, he goes all out, lovingly describing at great length the appearances of people and rooms. Already his psychological insight is acute, although some female characters are too stereotyped and conversations are sometimes artificial and stilted. However, the novel is rich with characters, imagery, ideas, and contrasting viewpoints. It is conspicuously a multifocal novel, employing an approach that was to become Dick's hallmark in his science fiction of the 1960s.

The main character, Stuart Hadley, is a television salesman, married to a woman whom he sees as a vegetable: "she was a generative principle, not a person. She was rooted, planted. A ripe, moist melon within panes of glass. As sweetened and fattened as any kept prostitute, made complacent by her blanket of respectability." Hadley begins to feel that life is meaningless and random: "A universe of chance . . . random particles swirling and settling without meaning." *Solar Lottery* is a literalization of this existential complaint.

When Hadley meets the hard and machinelike Marcia Frazier, editor of the racist, neo-fascist literary quarterly *Anima*, he naturally falls in love with her. She is described as a succubus, reptilian, but beautiful with an androgynous appeal. Her body is straight and firm like a boy's, unlike his full-breasted wife. In Jungian terms, it is a conflict between two archetypal forces in Hadley's psychology: the mother figure and the anima.

Another important figure is the power figure, Theodore Beckheim, the elderly black leader of a cult of purity called the Society of the Watchmen of Jesus. He becomes a father figure to Hadley, and an initiator into a kind of psychological death and rebirth experience. Beckheim preaches a doctrine of divine immanence: God *is* every physical manifestation in the universe, and the profane world will be transformed into the divine. The time is moving to a vast showdown between cosmic forces, and man must choose (as in *The Cosmic Puppets*). Beckheim wants to lead his people out of the cities (which are controlled by the war god, the Devil), back to the mountains. Despite his extremism, Beckheim articulates certain ideas that will reappear in Dick's own later philosophical writings. Here, as elsewhere, the power figure attracts and repels simultaneously. Dick endows Beckheim and later such other leaders as Molinari in *Now Wait for Last Year* with vision and ideas—a credible source for their power.

When Hadley learns that Marsha is having an affair with Beckheim, he feels that "in him was the possibility, the energy to annihilate himself and his tiny universe." When later she falls in love with Hadley, he becomes the hard metallic one, raping her, then beating her up. After some drunken adventures, he injures and blinds himself. This nightmarish episode constitutes the fantastic element of the book and gives it something in common with Dick's science fiction.

Dick never leaves his people in the pit. Hadley has spent his rage. He and his wife move to a new town and he sets up a tool repair and rental business—a service occupation that restores peace to his life.

### Gather Yourselves Together

The next mainstream novel was probably *Gather Yourselves Together,* also written in the early 1950s. It takes place in 1949 in postrevolutionary China and concerns three Americans—two men and a woman—who have remained to hand over control of a factory to the new government. One of the men, Carl, a boyish innocent, falls in love with the woman, Barbara, who is cold and emotionally repressed, and happens to be the ex-lover of Vern, the other man. She seduces Carl, using him as Vern used her, as if in revenge. The working out of this triangular situation is told rather tediously, with many flashbacks to minor incidents. The subplot of the political takeover of the factory is not well integrated with the romantic theme. Despite the vividness of some scenes, there is a meandering slackness to this novel, undoubtedly the weakest of Dick's mainstream works.

## *Mary and the Giant*

Evidently completed in 1955, but not published until 1987, *Mary and the Giant* revolves around a subject close to Dick's heart, music. Almost everybody in the novel is related somehow to the music business; music is the constant topic of conversation and is usually playing in the background. Joe Schilling, the "giant" of the title, is a record-shop proprietor who represents a taste for the classical, while Mary Ann Reynolds, a young woman whom he hires as a sales clerk, gravitates to jazz.

Mary is full of life and intelligence, with a bold, direct manner. Her experimental attitude toward life fits her preference for jazz, and she has an affair with the black jazz singer Carleton Tweany. But Tweany, however soulful, is a sellout: he is not above singing such songs as "*White* Christmas" or sleeping with sluttish white women like Beth Coombs, Joe's ex-wife.

In this novel the familiar pattern of the older man who falls in love with the younger woman recurs, as Joe fastens on Mary as an anima figure. Mary, for her part, projects upon Joe a kindly, "God the Father" image. When they make love, she overcomes her frigidity and has her first orgasm. After opening up to Joe, she quickly withdraws in reaction, becoming "a hard, chipped, highly polished device that seemed to have no particular feelings" (chap. 20)—an image of the android. Despite her assertive, dominating personality, she is as insecure and fearful as a little girl.

Mary lives in a world that is poorly thrown together, in which she is not comfortable—always changing jobs, residences, and men. She is compulsive and chronically restless. Joe sees that the problem is not within Mary: "she had not gone wrong; she was as right as anybody else and far more right than some . . . but still no way remained by which she could live. It was not a moral issue. It was a practical issue. Someday, in a hundred years, her world might exist. It did not exist now. He thought that he saw the new outlines of it. She was not completely alone, and she had not invented it as a single-handed effort. Her world was partially shared, imperfectly communicated" (chap. 21). Joe realizes that she is not at home in her world, and the only way she can succeed is to be free to be herself, to be let alone. Even his love, his attempts to help her were interfering with this. So he gracefully lets her go; by misleading her father and fiancé about her whereabouts, he gives her time to leave town with a jazz piano player whose "bop" stylings harmonize with her temperament. They move to San Francisco, she has a baby, and begins to lead a normal life—it is as if she has finally joined the human race after many desperate, driven years.

A very strong example of Dick's mainstream writing, *Mary and the Giant* is a tight, well-constructed narrative. The character of Mary is convincing and compelling. Although "cold" on the surface, she is a multilayered creation with whom the author empathizes strongly. Her refreshing honesty and directness are seductive. The scenes in the jazz club called The Lazy Wren, the wild party in Tweany's apartment, the sordid and claustrophobic atmosphere of Mary's family's home, and the well-drawn subsidiary characters make this novel memorable.

## The Broken Bubble

*The Broken Bubble* (originally titled *The Broken Bubble of Thisbe Holt*) was apparently completed in 1956. It is an effective exploration of the psychological subtleties of a four-way relationship. Jim Briskin, a classical music radio announcer, still in love with his ex-wife Pat, introduces her to a teenage couple, Art and Rachael. Pat becomes involved with the violent and possessive Art. Meanwhile, in her curious, willful way, Rachael falls in love with Jim. Pat goes through a psychotic episode, brilliantly depicted, as when she attempts suicide: "She picked up her brush and put the tip of it into the paint. In the darkness of the apartment she painted; she put more darkness around her. She lifted darkness and carried it about the living room and the bedroom and into the bathroom and the kitchen. She took it everywhere. She brought it to each thing in the apartment, and after that she turned it to herself." Jim rescues her, and they reunite, as do Art and Rachael. What is more, the four remain friends. This "happy" ending, far from seeming contrived, is fitting and well earned.

The "broken bubble" of the title refers to a minor incident in which one Thisbe Holt rolls around naked inside a plastic bubble at an optometrists' convention. After she leaves, the optometrists take the empty bubble and roll it back and forth among them, working up to a frenzy, then fill it with junk and throw it off the hotel roof. The episode impinges randomly on the lives of the principal characters when Art is falsely accused by the police of committing the act. But the broken-bubble image is suggestive also of the bubbles of ego that

Jim, Pat, Art, and Rachael all float in, that separate them in their relationships. During the course of the novel these bubbles are broken.

At the end, Jim is committed to helping protect the young couple from the harsh, uncaring forces in the world that must be opposed—represented here by the optometrists, the police, a political extremist named Grimmelman, and a used-car dealer named Looney Luke (who reappears in *The Simulacra*) with a particularly irritating advertising campaign. Luke's hysterical, insane laugh, broadcast throughout the city by a sound truck, permeating every building, is a powerful image of the cruel and irrational exploitative mentality. Jim is quietly heroic in refusing to read Looney Luke's ads on the radio, and this spirit extends to his holding out, in the face of her self-destructiveness, for the woman he loves.

## *Puttering about in a Small Land*

The title of the next realist novel, written in 1957, refers to the "small land" of Roger Lindahl's TV repair shop. His wife, Virginia, is ambitious, and ends up taking control of the business and expanding it into a large appliance store; but she, as much as Roger or any of the other characters, exists in the small land of her own mind. California, the land of opportunity which had lured the Lindahls from the East Coast, is small in its own way: the deadening conventionality of 1950s manners and morals contract the range of human happiness there as elsewhere.

In confronting the crash of his great expectations for finding the good life in California, Roger experiences a vision of the massive evils of the earth. He is revolted by the omnipresence of filth, decay, and moral degeneration:

He had a vision of crooks, swindles of every kind; he saw up into the office buildings and the crooked activity going on, the wheels, the machinery. . . . he saw the war itself as a stupendous snow-job, men killed for fat bankers to float loans, ships built that went right to the bottom, bonds that could not be redeemed, Communism taking over, Red Cross blood that had syphilis germs in it. Negro and white troops living together, nurses that were whores, generals who screwed their orderlies, profits and blackmarket butter, training camps in which recruits died by the thousands of bubonic plague, illness and suffering and money mixed together, sugar and rubber, meat and blood, ration stamps, V-D posters, short-arm inspections, M-1 rifles, USO entertainers with corks up their asses, motherfuckers and fairies and niggers raping white girls . . . he saw the sky flash and drip; private parts shot across the heavens, words croaked in his ears telling him about his mother's monthlies; he saw the whole world writhe with hair, a monstrous hairy ball that burst and drenched him with blood . . . (chap. 8)

This paranoid's feast of horrors defines the unpredictable outside world that Roger is trying to shut out, as well as the dangerous emotions he is repressing. The fantastic image at the end of the passage seems like something out of one of Dick's science-fiction novels; indeed, the whole catalogue anticipates the entropic landscapes of *Martian Time-Slip* and *Ubik*.

Into this wasteland a fertilizing influence appears: the familiar anima, in the person of Liz Bonner. Others consider her "dumb" and "scatterbrained"; Roger finds her refreshingly uninhibited and sensual, and a decided antidote to his cold and brittle wife. Liz is open about talking about sex and acting on her desires. He quickly becomes obsessed with her. One of Dick's most memorable characters, she is as spontaneous and changeable as the weather. Her attention is constantly shifting. One chapter, which takes place when she and Roger are in bed together, is entirely given over to her point of view, often veering into dreamlike stream-of-consciousness images. She sees sex as a way of transcending time: "When I am like this, she thought, I don't get old. As long as I am lying here, holding him inside me, I neither sink nor fall. I do not go in any direction. I am simply me. As long as I want. As long as I can keep him here" (chap. 17). Frequently she thinks of Virginia getting old while she and Roger lie clasped in the immortality of sexual union. She imagines Roger returning home and finding Virginia "only a dried-up crone. And when he asked her who she was, *she did not remember*" (chap. 17). Dick admired Molly Bloom's interior monologue in Joyce's *Ulysses*, and there is something of Molly in Liz. They are both amoral personifications of the archetypal feminine; their thoughts and words flow freely like a river. But for Roger, Liz's sexuality is as dangerous as it is enlivening. There is something maternally devouring about it: "I'm the one who will never wear out. I am here forever, lying here on the ground, holding you down where I can reach you and get at you and inside you" (chap. 17). He realizes finally that she is "a kind of ultimate being" with a "perfect core of unchangeability" (chap. 22). He cannot have a real relationship with her or ever really "have" her. She takes him out of himself, but she is not herself moved.

When Virginia discovers their affair, she exacts swift vengeance: with her mother in tow, she charges into Liz's house, humiliating Roger by catching him naked in Liz's bedroom. She forces him to transfer his store to her name, and quickly proves herself his superior in the man's world of business. He is relegated to puttering in the store basement in the evenings. Defeated by his wife in the area of his male pride and by his mistress on the emotional front, he finally escapes for Chicago with a new vision of freedom.

*Puttering about in a Small Land* shows mastery of in-depth characterization and narrative technique. In its concentration on the triangle of Roger, Liz, and Virginia, it fully develops the psychological dynamics of marital and extramarital relations that Dick returns to frequently in his later novels. It is a theme that obsesses him, and his empathy with all the parties involved is apparent—even the "bad wife" character. He takes care to show Virginia's point of view with remarkable lack of bias, though one cannot help but feel that Liz was right: Virginia is going to end up a dried-up crone because she cannot love.

## *In Milton Lumky Territory*

The next realist novel, evidently written in 1958, is a concise, ironic story, set in Idaho, of the marriage of a young man to his former fifth-grade teacher, and his devastating experiences in trying to run her business. Dick wrote *In Milton Lumky Territory* under the influence of Arthur Miller's *Death of a Salesman*. Both works deal with the tragedy of the common man, making the point, as Dick quoted in an interview, that "attention must be paid to this man."[1] Milton Lumky, a dumpy, red-faced salesman with a penchant for outrageous remarks, is not the main character in the novel, but he has center stage whenever he is on. Like Willy Loman, he is a man of essential goodness who has been beaten down by what he has come to see as the degrading nature of his job. The other characters are in his territory of influence; they are forced to acknowledge his struggles as not unrelated to their own.

Kim Stanley Robinson writes that in this work Dick fully expresses the theme that business relations under American postwar capitalism have a destructive effect on personal relations.[2] Bruce Stevens, the protagonist, deserts Lumky when he is seriously ill in order to make a business deal. He later realizes, after Lumky dies, that the salesman had been his only friend. When the deal turns out to have been a bad one, Bruce's wife Susan, the owner of the retail typewriter supply business that he manages, has to fire him, which strains their relationship. There is no evidence, however, to suggest that Dick's main intent is to indict the system. The system is, as always, within us, and Bruce's problems are caused more by his hubris and lack of ethical perspective than by external forces.

Bruce's standards are those of the discount-buying house he is working for at the beginning of the book. The emphasis is on reaping high profits by buying cheap merchandise regardless of quality and bypassing the service-oriented small retailer. When Bruce marries Susan, he finds himself managing the type of service-oriented enterprise that is antithetical to his values. But he approaches the management of it as a discount buyer would, driving thousands of miles to find a bargain on some foreign-made typewriters. His discount mentality causes him to blunder and fail to notice that they have non-standard keyboards.

Bruce has been riding for a fall by marrying the very woman who caused him humiliation as a child; as his teacher, she brought him up short on several occasions for his bullying tendencies. She remains his teacher and his conscience after they marry, for she will not permit him to unload the useless typewriters under false pretenses. She acutely points out to him that he has always envied his brilliant, successful older brother, and as a result has not learned enough about himself to develop a meaningful value system. And it is unclear in this novel that he ever does.

Milton Lumky diagnoses Bruce's malaise as lack of ability to love. When he tells him that he is caught up in selfish, materialistic goals and needs to develop some spiritual values, Bruce can only laugh helplessly. Despite Bruce's and Susan's lack of appreciation of the salesman's true character, Lumky goes out of his way to help them, even giving them money. His personal tragedy is that he must continue roaming the highways of Idaho in what he considers a degrading occupation. He faces his own unhappiness with ruthless candor, but this does not stop him from exhibiting a rough kindness to others. Bruce and Susan are insensitive to it; that is their tragedy.

Milton Lumky's Idaho is a provincial world of small towns, small minds, and a certain unrelieved nastiness. The images are suggestive: Bruce's hometown is filled with an acrid air and "clouds of sharp-winged yellow flies" that smash against windshields (chap. 1). His parents' home is a "tall gray ancient farmhouse, with dry soil around it, the weeds and geraniums growing out of the bare brown earth. No lawn. No green to speak of . . ." (chap. 8). The height of glory in this

society is epitomized by Bruce's brother Frank: "Going steady with
Ludmilla Meadowland, the blonde whom the senior class had elected
Miss Montario for the JC pageant of 1948. In the parade, on June
tenth, she had coasted down Hill Street on a float made of potatoes,
carrying a banner reading WIN MONTARIO HIGH WIN WIN. The
Principal of Montario High had shaken hands with both her and Frank,
and the picture of the three of them had appeared in the *Gazette* . . ."
(chap. 4).

The only reprieve from the dreariness of this barren land and culture
is to be found in the felicities of the heart. Bruce and Susan find happiness at the end when they move to Denver, out of Milton Lumky
territory, but if they have surpassed the deadness of Idaho, they have
lost something, too. Their comfortable life lacks the passion and commitment to self-knowledge that Lumky exemplified.

## Confessions of a Crap Artist

*Confessions of a Crap Artist,* written in 1959, was finally published
in 1975, the first of Dick's mainstream novels to appear in book form.
In many ways it is probably the best: its multifocal narration offers
inside glimpses into the minds of two of Dick's most fascinating characters—the "crap artist" Jack Isidore and his sister Fay Hume. The
novel derives its energy from the juxtaposition of their radically different perspectives.

Jack had been the classic "nerd" in high school, with his skinny
body, silver-framed glasses, dandruff, acne, and preoccupation with
science-fiction comics and pulp magazines. He was obsessed with pseu-
doscience and adolescent power fantasies which, if anything, have in-
tensified as he has grown into his thirties. Though devoid of scientific
training, he considers himself a scientist; he is continually clipping
articles, taking notes on unusual scientific facts, and compiling tables
of minutiae. His voice is one of absolute assurance mixed with complete ignorance:

Today in the 1950s, everyone's attention is turned upward, to the sky. Life
on other worlds preoccupies people's attention. And yet, any moment, the
ground may open up beneath our feet, and strange and mysterious races may
pour out into our very midst. It's worth thinking about, and out in California,
with the earthquakes, the situation is particularly pressing. Every time there's
a quake I ask myself: is this going to open up the crack in the ground that
finally reveals the world inside? Will this be the one? (chap. 1)

The full irrationality of Jack's inner world never breaks out, for he is so emotionally stunted that he can only maintain himself as an island, in and of and for himself. Significant communication with others is impossible; nobody can relate to his crazy ideas. However, Fay and her husband Charlie take him into their home after he gets in trouble for stealing a can of chocolate-covered ants to see if they can be brought back to life.

Dick based the idea for Jack Isidore's character on Isidore of Seville, who in the seventh century compiled the shortest encyclopedia ever written; it set down all knowledge available at the time in only thirty-five pages. Jack collects specious bits of knowledge, from which he spins fantasies that he cannot distinguish from fact. He quickly becomes involved with a group of UFO occultists in Fay's community, who concoct a theory that the world will end on a certain date, but the chosen few will be rescued by a flying saucer.

Despite all this, Dick sympathizes with the character for his complete lack of preconceptions such as those labored under by the rest of us: "I am amazed to see how, below the surface of gabble which he prattles constantly, he has a sort of shrewdly appraising subconscious which sees maybe very darkly into events . . . Maybe he doesn't just see as well as we do, but in fact—incredibly, really—somehow and somewhat better."[3] Indeed, Jack is an acute observer of others. He understands the reasons behind the conflicts in his sister's relationship with Charlie, as well as the manipulativeness with which she tempts Nat Anteil, a young student, away from his wife. Even Jack's semi-pornographic account of the affair, which he reads to Charlie, is written not out of vindictiveness, but out of a conscientiousness to his mission as a "scientist" to observe and report the facts.

Fay Hume plays the role of the anima-temptress, as did Liz Bonner in *Puttering about in a Small Land*. Like her, Fay is impulsive, uninhibited, outspoken, and even more aggressively sexual. But the root of her attractiveness lies in her ability to live in the moment with a seeming intensity and freedom. As Nat reflects:

As they drove along she spotted so many things that he missed . . . she lived so much more fully. Of course, she lived only in the present. And she had no ability to reflect. Or, for that matter, to read thoroughly or to contemplate. She had a limited span of attention, like a child. But, unlike a child—very unlike a child—she had the ability to pursue a goal over a long period of time . . . and once again he found himself wondering. How long a period? Years? All her life? Does she ever give up, when she wants something? (chap. 11)

Her sense of adventurousness and ability to take risks combines with an amoral willingness to manipulate and use the men who fall in love with her. She puts them in a double-bind because although she uses all her power to get them to do exactly what she wants, she despises them for being weak. Charlie, though a "macho" type, cannot cope with her contradictory needs. He sees her finally as a "devouring bitch" (chap. 8) and tries to kill her, but he fails and kills himself instead.

Fay is the most fascinating of all Dick's women because she combines the aspects of the recurrent types we find in his other novels: the bitch-wife and the sexually irresistible young woman. Nat is conscious of his helpless attraction to her vitality and siren sexuality even while being trapped in the spiderweb of her selfish purposes. She is a bundle of contradictions. Jack astutely sees that she has never accepted her own identity as a woman, and thus cannot fundamentally accept a man's love. Lest we be tempted to judge her, however, Dick puts us inside her head for a couple of chapters to see that she is a vulnerable human being and not just a castrating bitch. Furthermore, she can be outrageously funny, as when she tells off her psychiatrist: "My reputation in this town is going to be ruined. You never lived in a small town; it's easy though for you to say, living in San Francisco. You can screw anybody you want and nobody gives a damn. Up here they're voting on you in the PTA before you have your pants zipped back up" (chap. 15).

Gregg Rickman points out that *Confessions* is the first novel in which Dick mastered the "multi-character tangentially linked plot."[4] The point of view switches back and forth from Jack to Fay to Charlie, all in the first person, to a third-person narrator who dips in and out of various characters' thoughts. Those narrators who are most unbalanced and least reliable in the story are also those whose voices we hear. This approach is more successfully used to integrate the various points of view in Dick's later novels, which are characterized by a consistent multifocal, third-person interior viewpoint that allows him maximum flexibility in exploring the inner perceptual and emotional lives of his characters.

## The Man Whose Teeth Were All Exactly Alike

Written in 1960 and first published in 1984, *The Man Whose Teeth Were All Exactly Alike* was Dick's personal favorite among his mainstream novels. Like its predecessor, it is set in a small town in West

Marin County, California. The focus is on two men and their marriages: Leo Runcible, a local real estate agent, and his alcoholic wife Janet; and Walt Dombrosio, a commercial designer, whose wife Sherry embodies all of Fay Hume's bad qualities without any of her redeeming humor. The book's title refers to a fake Neanderthal skull that Dombrosio plants in order to humiliate his enemy, Runcible, whom he sees as the source of all his miseries.

Runcible has plenty of faults: he is an ignorant blowhard, and his intolerance toward Dombrosio's black dinner guest precipitates their hostility. Yet he emerges as a kind of hero at the end, after his claims of an important archeological discovery have been exploded. For quite a while he cannot accept the decision of the scientists; he is determined that the skull should be authentic no matter what the evidence to the contrary. Investing the skull with his hopes for the development of the town, he finally uses the fake to change the real to good effect. Armed with the knowledge that the skull's malformed jaw was caused by the town's contaminated water, he buys out the water company to eliminate the health hazard. No one else in the novel does anything similarly admirable, although Janet, despite her wretched appearance and state of mind, does make fumbling attempts to stand by her husband.

Sherry Dombrosio, on the other hand, seems to go out of her way to make life hell for Walt. Systematically she finds the chinks in his ego armor and drills into them with malice. Walt's weakness stems from his alienation from what is real. He spends long hours each day commuting and working at a job that is dedicated to the manufacture of appearances: designing packages for foods and other consumer goods. He and another man often indulge in "the fanciful consumption of the non-existent contents of their containers. Some days it was beer; other days they ate invisible cereal, ice cream, frozen vegetables, smoked pretend cigarettes—once, even presented the receptionist with a pair of nylon stockings that she could not see. Land of make-believe . . ." (chap. 2). That sums up his life in the work world. There is nothing deeper, no soul in it. Yet he has invested all of his masculine pride in the role of playing breadwinner, which diminishes his self-awareness independent of that role.

As Sherry asserts her right to work outside the home, he feels threatened in his masculinity and, as it happens, quits in a huff when his boss hires her. He denigrates his wife's qualifications: she "has a couple of cans in front and a nice flat fanny in back. And two long legs sticking out at the bottom. And a prestige voice" (chap. 8). After she has essentially taken his place in the man's world, her sexual supremacy is absolute. As Runcible observes, "She wears the pants in that family, and not only the pants; she's got what you usually find in the pants" (chap. 14). Sherry refuses to acknowledge Walt's hurt feelings as anything other than the remains of childhood neurosis. She answers his complaints about her usurping his natural role by saying he is projecting his insecurity on her; a veteran of psychoanalysis, she can always turn his attacks back on him.

Dombrosio retaliates by raping her. When she becomes pregnant and tries to arrange an abortion, he hits her with a chair. This show of strength miraculously subdues her, and she resolves to be a good wife from that point on, to resume her proper role at home, and to have his baby. A feminist reading would force one to conclude that Dick is hopelessly misogynistic, although perhaps not more so than Shakespeare in *The Taming of the Shrew*. Dick was not unaware of the problem: "It may be that one of the genuinely weak elements in my books is the female co-lead. I either romanticize them or paint them as harpies; I am not doing them justice by treating them with perspective. . . . I may have been so convinced that a good man can be ruined by a scheming woman on the make that I never got over it. Likewise VANITY FAIR. I may see all women as Becky Sharps or Amelias. God help me as a writer, then!"[5]

Nevertheless, there is psychological truth in Dick's portrayal of unhappy marriages, and he never exonerates from responsibility the husband whose weakness turns his wife into a harridan. In a way, Walt has created his own monster. And when he finally finds the strength to stand up for something of true significance—the life of his unborn child—he gains the power to change the monster into a sweet, submissive wife.

Dick claimed that in his mainstream novels he dealt in Jungian projections. The "real" world is a projection of inner states; the roles characters play in each other's lives are externalizations of inner selves. Whether this is any more true of the straight fiction than the science fiction, it is well to remember that the element of the fantastic pervades Dick's vision. It intrudes into *The Man Whose Teeth Were All Exactly Alike* in the plot surrounding the fake skull. But beyond that, as long as we are in Dick's world, be it realistic or science-fictional, we inhabit a psychic landscape where anything can happen and people are never to be taken at their face value. This is especially true of Dick's women. Their power to allure or persecute is by and large an endowment from his male characters. The women's recurrence as archetypal Jungian animas does not justify assigning misogynistic motives to the author. When he describes how women appear to men, he is talking about male psychology from the point of view of a man who loved women. He is not necessarily engaging in sexual politics.

## *Humpty Dumpty in Oakland*

The last of Dick's early realist novels, *Humpty Dumpty in Oakland* (completed in 1960), is an excellent book, full of ambiguities about interpretations of events in the story. We view these events mostly from the point of view of Al Miller, a used-car salesman who is discontented with his life. When Jim Fergusson, an older man who is like a father figure to him, sells the property Al's lot is on, Al becomes unhinged. He becomes convinced that Fergusson's friend Harman is a big-time crook and tries to warn Fergusson and his wife Lydia to avoid a real estate deal with the man (for property in Marin County—hardly a bad investment in 1960). The reader is so involved with Al's perspective that it is not clear till the end of the novel that the only con being perpetrated is Al's own deception of himself.

Al's friend Tootie calls him a "humpty dumpty"—someone who just perches and watches, letting life happen to him rather than exercising control. Al thinks he is in control, has power, when he tries to blackmail Harman, but his attempt is absurdly weak and wrongheaded. And Humpty has a great fall. When Al tries to leave California with some money Lydia has given him following Jim Fergusson's death, he is picked up by the police when she has second thoughts and is falsely accused of swindling the widow. His paranoid fantasy comes true—people are out to get him—but not in the way he imagined. He thought Harman was a crook who had one of Al's prize cars smashed and caused his wife Julie to lose her job. Actually, he discovers later, she quit her job, and juveniles were responsible for the vandalism—or so the responsible, objective voice of Lydia's lawyer informs us, if we can believe him.

To a large extent, Al acts unconsciously. He plays out his paranoid fantasies, believing until the end that Harman is out to get him. When Harman turns out to be magnanimous and forgiving, it only makes Al more desperate, and he turns vengeful and possibly suicidal. However, Al is saved at the last minute by Mrs. Lane, a black woman who intercedes like an angel and seductively takes him home with her: "Soon they were traveling through streets he had never seen before. Streets that he did not know" (chap. 16). The ending here, as in all of Dick's novels, promises a new beginning, and healing from the deepest emotional wounds. On the whole, Dick is allied with the comic vision rather than the tragic: there is always a saving grace.

We may see through Al's stupidities and misperceptions, but we are not inclined to judge him harshly. For Dick has not let us be complacent about what reality *really* is: there is no absolute certainty about how to interpret the novel's events. It is strongly suggested, however, that Al's construction of reality is mistaken, and until the end Al fights to preserve it because he doesn't want the shell of his ego, of his old life, to be broken. And yet it will break, like it or not. The ego shell cracks and perceptions are altered in strange ways—a link with a common pattern in Dick's science-fiction novels. In those and the mainstream novels alike the disorienting effects of psychological transformation and change are ever present.

# Chapter Four

# The Early Sixties

## The Man in the High Castle

Through 1960 Dick had already written at least twenty novels. *The Man in the High Castle,* brought out in 1962, was a dramatic breakthrough. Certainly the best novel he had written up to that time, it brought Dick his only Hugo Award, for best science-fiction novel of the year, awarded at the World SF Convention in 1963. Most readers of Dick would still rank it high on the list of his works. The basic premise is irresistible: that there is an alternate universe in which Germany and Japan won World War II. The characters are memorable and subtly drawn. Their lives touch tangentially in a fascinating dance. The narrative point of view switches among them, often in a stream-of-consciousness mode, in one of Dick's most successful uses of the multifocal technique. Philosophically, the book has proved deep enough to spark plenty of critical debate, and its use of the *I Ching* helped popularize that five-thousand-year-old Chinese oracle in America in the 1960s.

After winning the war, Germany and Japan partition the spoils, the Germans taking the East Coast of the United States, the Japanese taking the West Coast, with the Rocky Mountain states left as a neutral zone. The novel is primarily set in California, where the Japanese influence has proved to be a benign one. As represented by Mr. Tagomi, head of a trade mission in San Francisco, the Japanese are humane, conscientious rulers who are sickened by the genocidal Nazis, who continue to exterminate Jews and blacks whenever possible. The Japanese understand that as non-Aryans, they are susceptible to the same treatment. Tagomi serves as a cover for a clandestine meeting between representatives of peaceful factions from both countries, at which it is revealed that Germany is planning a preemptive nuclear attack on Japan. At the end one is left suspended: there is no guarantee that this can be averted, but there is hope.

Nazism represents unmitigated evil in the moral scheme of the novel. The root of its sickness is variously analyzed in psychological terms. As Baynes, the agent of the "good" German faction, muses, it is the cult of the individual taken to the extreme:

> They identify with God's power and believe they are godlike. That is their basic madness. They are overcome by some archetype; their egos have expanded psychotically so that they cannot tell where they begin and the godhead leaves off. It is not hubris, not pride; it is inflation of the ego to its ultimate—confusion between him who worships and that which is worshiped. Man has not eaten God; God has eaten man. (chap. 3)

This horrific image of reverse communion will be seen again in *The Three Stigmata of Palmer Eldritch,* where those who take Chew-Z, the drug of the evil "god" Palmer Eldritch, are themselves unknowingly consumed by it.

Another character, Juliana Frink, conceives a more Freudian explanation of the Nazis' insanity. They are "all committing incest, going back to the original sin of lusting for their own mothers. . . . like evil spores, the blind blond Nazi queens were swishing out from Earth to the other planets, spreading the contamination" (chap. 3). Yet she, too, is unconsciously attracted to that which she hates the most. The macho, heterosexual magnetism of Joe Cinnedella, an agent of the SD—the German secret police—disguised as an Italian truck driver, overrules her initial impression that he radiates death. She finds she must murder him to keep him from executing his mission of killing the novelist Hawthorne Abundsen.

Dick's Jungian analysis of the Nazi evil goes beyond the doctrine of Original Sin, whether Christian or Freudian. True, the Nazis ate the apple; they tried to be God. But the godhead they aspired to was the projection of their own egos, and as such was a mockery of spiritual attainment. They were possessed by the archetype of the Shadow—in their case, the dark side of the primitive Aryan blood religion that they idealistically denied—and unconsciously acted out its rites. While exalting part of their psyches to superhuman status, they plunged their true selves into the deepest abysm of ignorance. In their failure lies the danger of any idealism, religious or political, that makes an absolute value of a relative goal.

Tagomi, after hearing a review of the personality characteristics of the Nazi leaders, is physically sickened, so overcome with vertigo that he feels for a moment that he is dying. He later realizes that the Japanese can never "enter the monstrous schizophrenic morass of Nazi internecine intrigue" to ameliorate their policies (chap. 12). The Nazi way is cold and devoid of affective mentality, driven by a purely "realistic" rationalism. The Japanese, who have popularized the use of the *I Ching,* are sensitive to the balance of contrasting elements that structure each moment, and seek to align themselves with the cosmic purpose. This intuitive mysticism, however, is highly practical.

The *I Ching* interprets hexagrams constructed by the chance throw of coins or yarrow stalks to reveal the essence of a particular situation. The hexagrams are made up of yang and yin lines, either static or changing, constantly in the process of transformation into their opposite. Yang and yin, the two primal cosmic principles, correspond to the archetypal masculine and feminine. Yang is positive, active, light, and heavenly; yin is negative, receptive, dark, and earthly. The Tao is the synthesis of their interactions, the absolute amidst the flux of energies that radiate from these polar opposites and infinitely renew each other. The *I Ching* is more than a book: it is a physical manifestation of the Tao, and is animated by spirit. Most of the characters in the novel refer to it frequently to explicate the inner meaning of the crises they are experiencing.

Yang and yin are not synonymous, respectively, with good and evil, as has been sometimes thought. Dick himself muddies the waters by having Tagomi refer to the "Yin world in its most melancholy aspect" as "World of corpses, decay and collapse. Of feces. All that has died, slipping and disintegrating back down layer by layer. The daemonic world of the immutable; the time that was." Yang, on the other hand, is "empyrean, ethereal," a high castle of spirituality (chap. 14). But as Ursula Le Guin points out:

> In taoist thought, of course, the negative is not inferior to the positive, and yin is not "bad" while yang is "good." Yin is, however, dark, wet, low, passive, soft, etc.—all qualities that Western/technological civilisation neglects or contemns in favor of the yang qualities bright, dry, high, aggressive, hard, etc; yin is also, and this may be the important point, female.[1]

Thus yang and yin are two sides of a coin, and the "negativity" of yin connotes no more moral inferiority than the negative pole of a magnet possesses.

The Western way, which Nazism represents to a perverted extreme, is yang: the outward urge to know, master, and exploit. The Eastern way is yin: the inward stroke of consciousness, emphasizing self-knowledge. Neither is in itself sufficient to realize the organic inter-connection between individual consciousness and the life of everything else. The main characters in *High Castle* achieve wisdom by transcend-ing the duality of existence in the timeless truth of the Tao. The *I Ching* is a guide in this quest for wholeness.

In a kind of unconscious attempt at psychological balancing of yin and yang, the Japanese in *High Castle* display a peculiar obsession with the artifacts of American popular culture. Such relics of the prewar civilization as Mickey Mouse wristwatches, pictures of Jean Harlow, comic books, posters, and Civil War pistols fetch high prices on the collector's market. The Japanese have also created a market for fake artifacts that are virtually indistinguishable from the originals. As mas-ters of imitation themselves, they have adopted ersatz tastes in feeding off of the superficialities of an alien culture. Frank Frink, Julia's ex-husband, is at first employed by a company that produces fakes such as the ersatz Colt .44 with which Tagomi shoots two German SD agents. In that instance, it turns out to be much more important that the gun works than that it lacks true historicity—for Tagomi's spon-taneously right action saves the life of Baynes and possibly the peace of the world. He partakes of the Tao at that moment.

Robert Childan, dealer in the collectibles of his own conquered na-tion, is at the outset torn between yin and yang. He identifies with the German assertion of white supremacy, while fawning on the Japa-nese and seeing them as the perfect form of humanity. On either count, he is an unsympathetic character, being incoherent and intolerant. Yet he achieves a breakthrough—not through the *I Ching,* as with Tagomi and Juliana Frink—but through an abstract piece of American jewelry made by Frank Frink after he leaves the company that makes the fake Colt .44s. As a contemporary artifact, the jewelry would seem to be valueless, having no historicity. Furthermore, it is shapeless, lacking the form of conventional beauty. But Childan comes to appreciate its almost magical properties of *wu*—a word implying the balance of yin and yang in peaceful harmony: "The name for it is neither art, for it has no form, nor religion. . . . It is authentically a new thing on the face of the world" (chap. 11). If an object has *wu,* the whole question of its historical authenticity becomes unimportant.

The question of the authentic and the fake extends to the whole world of *High Castle.* In this fictional universe there exists a novel by Hawthorne Abundsen called *The Grasshopper Lies Heavy,* which is about an alternate world in which Germany and Japan *lose* World War II.

Juliana seeks out the subversive Abundsen to warn him that the Germans are trying to have him killed. Although reputed to live in an impregnable "high castle," Abundsen actually inhabits an ordinary single-story suburban home. During Juliana's visit she throws the *I Ching* and interprets the resulting hexagram "Inner Truth" to mean that the world Abundsen created in his novel is the true one and the one they live in is a forgery. This is further emphasized by the discovery that Abundsen used the *I Ching* to write *The Grasshopper Lies Heavy*. The inner truth of the oracle has passed into the fiction.

The reality of Abundsen's book differs in some essential aspects from our own. Roosevelt ends his term in 1940 and is succeeded by President Tugwell, who anticipates and takes precautions against the attack on Pearl Harbor. After the war, the British Empire extends over all of Europe. It is in some respects a better, more peaceful world than the one we know. But if the *I Ching* says it is real, is ours then fake? Which reality has ontological priority—ours, that of *High Castle,* or that of *Grasshopper*? Or are all these merely relative, and there is no authentic reality? As N. B. Hayles notes: "we too may be fictions . . . Dick uses his fiction-within-a-fiction-become-real-world to set up an equation: as we think the characters of *High Castle* are to us, so we are to reality.[2] Dick himself stated that Abundsen's creation was intended to be true only in essential substance, not in details.[3] Nevertheless, the implications about the potential fictionality of any objective reality remain in the text of *High Castle*.

After he kills the SD men, an act that violated his Buddhist beliefs about the sanctity of life, Tagomi looks for some resolution to his moral conflict: that he had to do evil to achieve good. He finds it in the piece of jewelry with *wu,* which temporarily transports him to the traffic-congested streets of a very different San Francisco than he knows—our own. He directly experiences an alternate reality, going beyond Hawthorne Abundsen, who merely wrote about it. Tagomi realizes: "We really do see astigmatically, in fundamental sense: our space and our time creations of our own psyche, and when these momentarily falter—like acute disturbance of middle ear" (chap. 14). For a moment, the distortion is suspended for him, and the world is revealed as it "really" is.

The resulting vision is what Dick calls the *koinos kosmos*—the transcendental, archetypal world full of strange transformations that exists behind the limited, individual perspective, the *idios kosmos*.[4] Beyond even that alternate reality lies the Tao: the ultimate reality, surpassing yet interpenetrating all polarities—good and evil, inner and outer, knowledge and ignorance, yin and yang. Evil, even that of the Nazis, is not an ontological absolute in *High Castle*. Dick allows a way for the "little man" to slip between the cracks in the clash of the mighty cosmic opponents, such as Ormazd and Ahriman in *The Cosmic Puppets*. Tagomi, Frank and Juliana Frink, Childan: these are the little people who somehow matter in the incomprehensibly vast scheme of things. Says Dick of Tagomi: "the positive little figure outlined against the universal rubble is . . . gnat-sized in scope, finite in what he can do . . . and yet in some sense great. I really do not know why. I simply believe in him, and I love him. He will prevail. There is nothing else. At least nothing else that matters. That we should be concerned about. Because if he is there, like a tiny father-figure, everything is all right."[5]

## *We Can Build You*

Beginning with *The Man in the High Castle*, Dick's science-fiction novels began to reflect the full power of his individual voice, which had been developing in his mainstream works. That voice is wry, ironic, philosophical, and introspective—one might add frequently depressed; it permeates the words and thoughts of most of his main characters. That is to say, the characters seem to reflect more than ever the point of view of somebody intensely interested in his own psychology and the ultimate questions of the universe—the author himself.

*We Can Build You* is a transitional work between the mainstream novels of the 1950s and the science fiction of the 1960s; the science-fictional element is de-emphasized in favor of psychological themes. Usually thought of as a later work, it was actually completed in 1962. Its first appearance was in *Amazing Stories* in November 1969 and January 1970, under the title "A. Lincoln, Simulacrum"; it included a final chapter written with Dick's consent by the magazine's editor, Ted White, who thought the novel lacked a proper conclusion. Dick had White's conclusion dropped, however, from the first book publication in 1972.[6]

Critics usually unfairly regard *We Can Build You* as an artistic failure because what seems to be the main plot of the book—the story of a company that produces simulacra, or lifelike androids of historical Civil War figures—bit by bit dissolves into exclusive focus on Louis Rosen's obsessive love for his partner's eighteen-year-old daughter, Pris

Frauenzimmer. Kim Stanley Robinson considers the book an example of one of Dick's "broken backed" novels—suffering from "his tendency to drop one plot in favor of another."[7] Certainly Dick will confound those expecting conventional narrative unity, for *We Can Build You* is an experimental novel masquerading as straight science fiction. As Louis, the narrator, descends into schizophrenia, the center of interest shifts from the projection of human life on the inanimate through building simulacra, to the search for authentic human feeling within oneself.

The image of the simulacrum is the key metaphor in the novel for the inner quest for reality. Pris (the eternal anima) fascinates Louis because she seems to lack the qualities of humanness with which she has endowed the simulacra she has invented:

As we walked back to the living room together I took a close look at her: I saw a little hard, heart-shaped face, with a widow's crown, black hair, and due to her odd make-up, eyes outlined in black, a Harlequin effect, and almost purple lipstick; the whole color scheme made her appear unreal and doll-like, lost somewhere back behind the mask which she had created out of her face. And the skinniness of her body put the capper on the effect: she looked to me like a dance of death creation animated in some weird way, probably not through the usual assimilation of solid and liquid foods . . . perhaps she chewed only walnut shells. (chap. 3)

Her sexuality becomes even more potent with her hardness and artificiality. Even as Louis falls under her spell, he realizes that she is incapable of love and true feeling for others. She sees others as hollow shells, just as she sees herself. In effect, she has populated her world with simulacra. She pours herself into the creation of a simulacrum of Abraham Lincoln, and perhaps loses her soul in the process. "We're like gods," she says, ". . . yet by giving them life we empty ourselves" (chap. 8).

Pris spurns Louis's love and takes up instead with Sam Barrows, a real estate magnate whose calculating, impersonal, ambitious drive mirrors her own. Under his Mephistophelian influence, she is transformed into the actress "Pristine Womankind"—more archetypal and emotionally inaccessible than ever. Barrows wants to populate his tract houses on the moon with simulacra, to give the illusion of human habitability to a hostile, alien environment. In *Martian Time-Slip* and *The Three Stigmata of Palmer Eldritch* Dick will depict colonies on Mars as dreary, dehumanizing places whose promise of escape from the problems of Earth is similarly illusory.

The simulacra are not mere automata but self-contained "homeostatic systems." They are cut off from their environment and are not dependent upon an operator outside of themselves. They possess consciousness and free will. When the Lincoln simulacrum is "born," he suffers pain, fear, and separation from a certain primal unity. Later he exhibits a tendency to brood over his lost love, Ann Rutledge, and a liking for reading aloud from *Winnie the Pooh* and *Peter Pan*. Lincoln engages Barrow in a debate about what it means to be human and proves, with reference to Spinoza, that if humans have no souls, as Barrows holds, there is no essential difference between men, machines, and animals. In other words, the simulacra are as human as Pris and Barrow, if not more so. The machines are not as emotionally homeostatic as the people, whose emotional isolation renders their own feelings mechanical.

A further loss of feeling may be found in the larger society of *We Can Build You*. All school children are screened for schizophrenia, and one in four is sent to a mental health clinic. The official diagnostic test is, however, skewed to a dull and conventional norm of sanity. The "correct" answer to the meaning of the proverb "A rolling stone gathers no moss" is "A person who's unstable will never acquire anything of value" (chap. 17).

Louis himself, driven mad by Pris, is diagnosed as having "Magna Mater" schizophrenia by a famous psychiatrist:

"Now, the Magna Mater, the form you have, was the great female deity cult of the Mediterranean at the time of the Mycenaean Civilization. Ishtar, Cybele, Attis, then later Athene herself . . . finally the Virgin Mary. What has happened to you is that your anima, that is, the embodiment of your unconsciousness, its archetype, has been projected outward, onto the cosmos, and there it is perceived and worshiped." (chap. 17)

Thus through Pris, the Great Mother who gives both life and death, Louis experiences all possible oppositions: warmth and coldness, love and hate, creativity and analytical destructiveness. And as long as these inner conflicts are externalized and projected onto her, he cannot transcend them and regain his sanity.

At the end, he manages to overcome his obsession with Pris through controlled fugues induced by hallucinogenic drug therapy. But the real Pris is left alone in a mental health clinic, "carding and weaving virgin black sheep's wool, utterly uninvolved, without a thought for me or for any other thing" (chap. 18). In her own schizophrenic state, she is too far removed from external life to want to change. She remains an archetypal figure, like a Fate, weaving her webs of illusion to delude and ensnare the Dickian hero.

## Martian Time-Slip

Dick followed up the distinctive achievement of *The Man in the High Castle* with an equally brilliant novel, *Martian Time-Slip*. This one, however, did not find a hardcover publisher, as did its predecessor. After a 1963 serialization in *Worlds of Tomorrow* under the title "All We Marsmen," it was finally published as a Ballantine paperback in 1964. It sold poorly and quickly passed into obscurity, not to be reprinted until 1976, when Dick's reputation resurged. Dick stated that the novel's failure deterred him from continuing the artistic evolution that had gained impetus from the success of *High Castle*.[8] As a result, he went back to writing somewhat more conventional novels, such as *The Game-Players of Titan*, *The Simulacra*, and *The Penultimate Truth*. Since masterpieces such as *The Three Stigmata of Palmer Eldritch* and *Dr. Bloodmoney* were also written in this period of the early 1960s, however, it may be seen that the setback was a minor one.

In *Martian Time-Slip* Dick effectively utilizes multifocal viewpoints to comment on the nature of the schizophrenic experience and its implications for our evaluation of "normal" experience. One focal character is Arnie Kott, the rich, ruthless head of the plumbers' union on Mars. He is a no-nonsense opportunist who tries to exploit the precognitive schizophrenic boy, Manfred Steiner, in order to get information pertaining to an investment decision. Manfred, into whose mind the narrative sometimes strays, sees the inverse of the stable, commonsense reality known to Arnie. Manfred's world is entropic: it is in continual decline, as the horrifying spirit of the Gubbler pervades everything, reducing all communication to meaningless "gubble" and all life to dust and rot. The third main viewpoint character is Jack Bohlen, who stands astride the worlds of Arnie and Manfred. A borderline schizophrenic himself, he nevertheless functions competently as a repairman in the real world. Arnie employs him to build a machine to communicate with Manfred. Jack is on one hand drawn into Arnie's world, even sharing his mistress Doreen, while on the inside he is being infected by Manfred's diseased imagination.

Manfred is a beautiful, graceful boy who dances about to the rhythms of an inner music. But he is autistic, split off entirely from interpersonal relations. As Jack realizes, Manfred can only see the destructive aspect of life:

Now I can see what psychosis is: the utter alienation of perception from the objects of the outside world, especially the objects which matter: the warm-hearted people there. And what takes their place? A dreadful preoccupation with—the endless ebb and flow of one's own self. The changes emanating from within which affect only the inside world. It is a splitting apart of two worlds, inner and outer, so that neither registers on the other. Both still exist, but each goes its own way. (chap. 11)

Manfred's morbid introspectiveness leads not to self-knowledge but to self-contraction to a tiny core of identity besieged by hostile forces. This paranoia is rooted in the fear that his deepest self will prove to be the ultimate horror. All human beings have within them a "gubbish worm" made of "wet, bony-white pleats" (chap. 8); such functions as eating and sex are driven by that putrescent essence.

Manfred innocently projects his deranged vision so powerfully on others that they begin to see things the way he does, particularly Jack, who has suffered his own schizophrenic episodes in which he saw other people as mechanisms. Under the influence of Manfred, Jack sees Doreen deteriorate before his eyes as he tries to make love to her:

Bending over her he saw her languid, almost rotting beauty fall away. Yellow cracks spread through her teeth, and the teeth split and sank into her gums, which in turn became green and dry like leather, and then she coughed and spat up into his face quantities of dust. The Gubbler had gotten her, he realized, before he had been able to. So he let her go. She settled backward, her breaking bones making little sharp splintering sounds. (chap. 10)

The vision proceeds even more graphically until everything dissolves in an insane babble: "The Gubbler is here to gubble gubble you and make you into gubbish" (chap. 10). This scene, replayed several times through Manfred's nonchronological time-sense, is the most viscerally terrifying in Dick. Equally disturbing will be the implications advanced in such works as *Three Stigmata* and "Faith of Our Fathers" that God himself is the arch-gubbler—objectively, not merely subjectively, speaking.

As in *We Can Build You*, there is a sense in *Martian Time-Slip* that schizophrenia is a pervasive, infectious disease. As Jack's father says, ". . . everybody seems to have it nowadays; it's common, like flu or polio used to be, like when we were kids and almost everybody caught measles. Now you have this. One out of three, I heard on TV, one time" (chap. 8). The cause of this epidemic, it is implied, is the increased dehumanization of life: an overpopulated Earth, through crowded cooperative apartment complexes and lack of freedom; on desolate Mars, through boredom and loneliness. The public schools are entirely run by simulacra, whose efficiency at indoctrinating children with mind-numbing, stereotyped attitudes far outstrips that of human teachers. The educational system has literalized its metaphorical mechanicalness. It is anti-intellectual and anti-individual. Subtly it splits the minds of its students, causing them to identify with the affectless machine and not the feeling organism. It in effect promotes the growth of schizophrenia, while teaching children to function in an insane society.

Schizophrenia is seen in this novel as a horror in which the dark shadowy fears and inner demons are let loose into the day world of ordinary consciousness. Yet Manfred is not evil in himself. He is the only one who can see the beauty and grace of the mysterious Bleekmen, the indigenous Martians, who resemble African bushmen. Correspondingly, Heliogabalus, Arnie's tame Bleekman, who can look telepathically into Manfred's mind, regards schizophrenics as visionaries:

"Who can say if perhaps the schizophrenics are not correct? Mister, they take a brave journey. They turn away from mere things, which one may handle and turn to practical use; they turn inward to *meaning*. There, the black-night-without-bottom lies, the pit. Who can say if they will return? And if so, what will they be like, having glimpsed meaning? I admire them."(chap. 6)

This positive perspective anticipates R. D. Laing's position in *The Politics of Experience* (1967) that the schizophrenic's voyage into the inner realms is "one of the forms in which, often through quite ordinary people, the light began to break through the cracks in out all-too-closed minds." However, Laing recognized that the journey entailed "many terrors, spirits, demons to be encountered, that may or may not be overcome."[9] Dick hardly soft-pedals the horrific aspects of the quest, but he plays with the possibility that the psychotic may sometimes glimpse reality more fully than "normal" people can. Manfred, for example, can see the future—but it is not encouraging. He experiences in advance the decay of his body in an old persons' home.

Manfred's ability to warp other people's perceptions recalls *Eye in the Sky* and its theme of the power of an individual to become the god of another person's reality. When Arnie relives a segment of his life through Manfred's time-altering power, he begins to perceive as the boy does. Suddenly the world is hostile. His secretary turns into a lascivious machine with sadistic teeth. The newspaper he tries to read quickly turns into gubble-gubble words. His paranoia makes him attempt to kill Jack Bohlen, whom Arnie imagines is responsible for all his problems. In doing so, he is shot by a Bleekman arrow and dies— but only in his hallucination. Then, when he gets transported back to his "sane" reality, he is killed again—this time for real—but dies thinking he is still trapped in one of Manfred's schizophrenic worlds. Having lost the ability to distinguish between illusion and reality, he is authentically psychotic himself. Sobered by Arnie's loss of a stable reference point in his evaluation of reality, Jack reflects: "It never occurred to me before how much our world is like Manfred's—I thought they were absolutely distinct. Now I see that it's more a question of degree" (chap. 16).

Dick questions the validity of the concept of objective reality through portraying altered states of consciousness—here schizophrenic, in other novels drug-induced. His point is not that there is no truth, but that we can't trust our perceptions. "Out there" is to some extent a reflection of what is "in here." This is not, strictly speaking, solipsism, the theory that only the self exists (unless "Self" be understood in the Eastern sense of universal consciousness). On the contrary, Dick is warning that if we isolate our consciousness from other people, as Manfred does, we will plunge into an even less desirable version of the dream that we call ordinary reality. Jack Bohlen, at the end of the novel, has become healed. He has returned to his wife after his affair with Doreen, and is last seen, reunited with his father, seeking to help Manfred's mother: "their light flashed here and there, and their voices could be heard, business-like and competent and patient" (chap. 16). The renewal of Jack's personality is one with his reintegration into the world of the living. Whether or not the world is real, we must live in it, and must be whole to do so.

## Dr. Bloodmoney

*Dr. Bloodmoney, or How We Got Along After the Bomb* was published in 1965, and owed its title to the inspiration of Stanley Kubrick's film *Dr. Strangelove, or How I Learned to Stop Worrying and Love the Bomb,* released in 1963. The novel was completed by early 1963, however, with the original title "In Earth's Diurnal Course" and has no relationship to the film other than the coincidental presence of a mad scientist and a nuclear war.

The first third of the novel takes places on the day nuclear bombs strike the San Francisco area; the rest is set years later in western Marin County, where a small community of survivors has adapted to the post-holocaust environment. There are severe problems: the great number of mutant births, the scarcity of food, the lack of modern communication or transportation. Despite these shortcomings, small-town life goes on as it always has. Several critics, namely Suvin, Jameson, and Robinson, see a utopian quality in Dick's West Marin world, a "vision of freshening our own stale and fallen universe, of a utopian revitalization of the tired goods and services all around us, their projection into some genuinely Jeffersonian commonwealth beyond the bomb. . . ."[10] This is grandiose; Dick may have had faith that humanity would continue to struggle along even in the worst eventuality, but the society in *Dr. Bloodmoney* does not recommend itself as an ideal, even if it is not as dystopian as most of his settings. Perhaps the most surprising feature of this world is how much life is proceeding as normal.

It is also surprising that Dr. Bruno Bluthgeld, the Dr. Bloodmoney of the title, is not a major character; he is important, but he is only one of nine personalities who serve as Dick's narrative foci, all of whom help define the total gestalt. Bluthgeld is a nuclear scientist whose miscalculation allowed bomb tests that caused widespread genetic damage. As a result, he is convinced that everyone is perpetually watching and judging him. After a world war nearly wipes out all civilization, his guilt becomes almost too intense to bear. His only friend, Bonny Keller, sees him as a man of conscience who is being scapegoated. She is wrong; Dick does not like this character, as he mentions in the book's Afterword,[11] and makes sure the reader understands that he *is* guilty.

At first it appears that Bluthgeld's guilt that he is responsible for the atomic devastation of San Francisco is a figment of his imagination. A true solipsist, he considers himself "the omphalos, the center, of all this cataclysmic disruption" (chap. 6). In his mind, he has responded to the hatred of others from the level of his collective unconscious. Without willing it, he has handed the world the fruit of its alienation of him. Having helped create the bomb, he thinks he has the mental power to detonate it as a reaction against the enemy, which in his vast paranoia is all of mankind.

Moving to West Marin, Bluthgeld assumes the name of Jack Tree and becomes a shepherd, hiding his true identity. But he is still a wolf in sheep's clothing. Eventually his paranoia comes to a head, and he wills a second holocaust. This time, the cause-effect relationship is clear. The bombs do start exploding again. His solipsism is verified by the author: this is Dr. Bloodmoney's world. He is its evil god, just as the characters in *Eye in the Sky* controlled the common reality of the others in that novel. Dick's implication is that people like Bluthgeld are not mere loonies; they have the power to warp reality to conform to their megalomaniac delusions. They are dangerous, even if they appear impotent and pathetic, as does Bluthgeld throughout most of the book. The power of thought is that immense. But Bluthgeld's power is limited. He is neither omnipotent nor the center of the universe, for after his death life goes on.

Bluthgeld is finally killed by a lesser evil god: the phocomelus Hoppy Harrington, a mutant without arms or legs, who has become a petty tyrant in West Marin due to his psychokinetic powers. Having built himself a kind of mechanical body, a cart that is wired to his brain, he sees himself as a kind of superman. The greater his power becomes, the more corrupt he becomes. Through the power of his mind he is slowly trying to murder Walt Dangerfield, who has become disk jockey for the world in his orbiting satellite, providing the scattered communities throughout the world with their principal unifying, humanizing influence. Hoppy, an excellent mimic, wants to usurp Dangerfield's place in the sky, continuing the broadcasts himself. He wants to attain symbolic godhood in lieu of the full humanity that his physical abnormality has not allowed him to obtain in his life. But despite his selfish, inflated ego, in a corner of his mind he still regards himself as a freak. Hoppy, says Dick, "epitomizes the monster in us:

the person who is hungry. Not hungry for food, but hungry for coercive control over others. This drive in Hoppy stems from a physical deprivation. It is compensation for what he lacked from birth. Hoppy is incomplete, and he will complete himself at the expense of the entire world; he will psychologically devour it."[12] Like the malevolent child Jory in *Ubik,* he is a personification of a blind, grasping, anti-evolutionary trend in human nature. His real deformity is spiritual, not physical.

In no way does Dick associate physical deformity with evil, for the character that triumphs over Hoppy is also a freak: Bill Keller, a mere homunculus growing in the side of his sister Edie, Bonny's child. His mental powers enable him to exchange bodies with another living being. When Hoppy psychokinetically removes him from Edie, he turns the tables on the phocomelus and takes over his body, leaving Hoppy to die in Bill's own body, which is no more than a tiny head.

Bill has the power to talk to souls who have died. They exist in some kind of half-life, awaiting rebirth into a new body, as they do also in *Ubik.* Though Bill is disgusted by "those old crummy, sticky dead" (chap. 13), there are intimations even here that all is not lost. As long as there is consciousness, there can be renewal: even after death, even after the bomb.

Bonny, who is one of the last remaining beautiful women, represents a regenerative, fertilizing influence. During the first bomb blast she rushes out of her house and makes love to a total stranger, as a result of which Edie and Bill are born. The psychiatrist Dr. Stockstill notes that "she makes the most of life in every contingency" (chap. 9). Sexually aggressive, she has many affairs, and is generally dissatisfied with the weakness of her lovers and her husband. These men seem to reflect the entropic state of the world. The hope for humanity lies in what the feminine can bring forth. In this case, Bonny's offspring redeem the distorted masculine psychology of power epitomized by Hoppy. For Bill Keller appropriates Hoppy's organic-mechanical form, and gives promise of using his powers for good.

*Dr. Bloodmoney* is notable for showing how each character subtly touches the lives of others. Everyone in the book can and does have the power to affect each other's universe, warp each other's everyday reality in many little ways. The post-holocaust setting has its greatest significance in presenting a community, a microcosm of humanity, forming a common reality as the sum of their mutual interexperience. Their interplay defines the struggle for balance of the psychic elements that they each represent. Each one embodies a case of one of the various problems of power, isolation, conformity, and independence from the group.

Of course, they are well-rounded characters, not mere abstractions; the human realism of the novel is in large part the reason for its success. All the characters are sympathetic, at least to some degree. No one is unflawed; all succumb to pettiness. The force of good arises, not from any single person, but from the universal tendency of life to persist and grow. It is as if we need them all—even Bluthgeld—to understand humanity. His paranoia and hatred are the ravings of a soul isolated from vivifying contact with others. His ignorance of the total reality is his evil, and his death is the compensation, the blood money, paid to the survivors of his madness.

## The Game-Players of Titan

Dick's next novel exhibited more of his characteristic humor than did *High Castle, Martian Time-Slip,* or *Dr. Bloodmoney,* which had serious themes and an identifiable sociological dimension. That may explain why they have been lauded by critics and works such as *The Game-Players of Titan* ignored and denigrated. *Game-Players* suffers by comparison because of its labyrinthine and often confusing plot. Dick never satisfactorily resolves the murder mystery intrigue that occupies the first part of the book, and deeper issues remain relatively undeveloped. Nevertheless, the novel partakes of the brilliance of the overall concept that extends through Dick's work of the 1960s.

The type of humor in the novel is evident from the first sentence: "It had been a bad night, and when he tried to drive home he had a terrible argument with his car." Automobiles and household appliances, thanks to something called the "Rushmore effect," can talk and are sometimes recalcitrant—just like ordinary nonverbal machines. Here as elsewhere in Dick, such mechanical devices parody the more rigid aspects of human behavior. The Rushmore effect can separate truth from reality, however, in a way ordinary human perception cannot: it can tell who is authentically human and who is a vug, or creature from Titan, in human form.

The vugs, whose natural form is that of amorphous, gelatinous blobs, have occupied Earth after winning a war in which humanity nearly managed to sterilize itself though radiation exposure. Vugs have the capability of controlling humans' minds or simulating their form, behavior, and memories. The details of this process are never made clear, nor is there an attempt to portray a human mind in the grip of alien possession in the manner of Manfred's nightmarish experiences in *Martian Time-Slip*.

The plot revolves around the game of Bluff, which is somewhat akin to Monopoly. To maximize the chances for fertile matches, mates are exchanged regularly through Bluff contests, and property rights are traded in the same manner. Winning players are known as "bindmen," with the status of medieval barons, holding absolute power over a specific area. The social system and chance method of distribution of power recalls *Solar Lottery*. As in that novel, the game here is rigged. The vugs, while seeming to try to increase the birthrate by establishing Bluff as a means of marital selection, are actually using their mental powers to keep humanity relatively infertile. But the true game in the novel is telling illusion from reality: who is the human and who is vug?

In attempting to make that vital distinction, Pete Garden, the schlemiel hero, is tied in knots, as is the reader—especially since some characters are only partially taken over by the vugs, or may not be aware that they are vugs. While under the influence of a combination of mind-altering drugs, which precipitate a psychotic episode, Pete sees Mary Anne McClain, the eighteen-year-old anima figure whom he finds irresistibly attractive, change into a vug. This turns out to be a paranoid hallucination. However, we may note in passing that the vision of one's beloved as an alien being, a cold, heartless *thing*, shows the anima's potential for negativity. The male who projects a fantasy-image on a woman is likely to make an enemy of her inner nature.

Mary Anne has a psychokinetic ability that cannot be predicted by others with precognitive psi powers. Her talent is acausal, following Jung and Pauli's synchronicity principle, which postulates phenomena that are out of the cause-effect stream of events. She is able to kill her father and mother, who have been taken over by vugs, because she can act in ways that their causally bound precognitive powers cannot foresee. She represents the variable element that Dick, from the time of "The Variable Man," sees as hopeful and positive. In a game of Bluff with the vugs, she helps Pete and his team win by counteracting the vugs' psychokinetic powers, which the vugs have used to change the values of cards dealt—a kind of cheating that is part of their rules of the game.

After the vugs lose, in desperation they alter the humans' realities and thrust them into a vacuous darkness. The humans are separated as if in a psychosis, utterly isolated, unable to apprehend each other except as vague, menacing presences. During this episode Mary Ann sees the vugs from their own perspective, as luminous beings, weightless, free from the crushing gravity of Earth, which contains the waning race of humans: "Stunted, alien creatures, warped by enormous forces into miserably malformed, distorted shapes" (chap. 17). When she upholds the human point of view as having equal validity, she is told by a vug: "Ideally . . . both views can be made to coincide. However, in practicality, that does not work" (chap. 17). As a rule, Dick doesn't try to make incompatible points of view coincide: his use of multifocal narration allows juxtaposition of radically different perspectives in their purity, undiluted by reduction to a common consensual reality. Even the vugs have a right to have their viewpoint represented.

The unpleasant vugs parallel the abysmal super-beings in some of Dick's later fiction, particularly *The Three Stigmata of Palmer Eldritch.* At the same time they are comic (on Earth they take names like U. S. Cummings and E. B. Black; humans can easily eject them from their apartments by use of "vug sticks"). The problem of the alien here, as in science fiction in general, is that it represents some human potential that is rejected or unrealized. Comedy helps make more palatable the confrontation with the terrible otherness of the vug, whose form suggests some king of primal, vital, plasmic life energy. The vugs withhold the gift of life from humanity because, in a sense, humans have shirked conscious recognition that, on a deeper level, they themselves are the aliens.

## *The Simulacra*

Dick's next novel, *The Simulacra,* is a grab bag of almost all of the themes and character types found in his other novels. Everything is here: a repressive police state, a ruling elite in conflict with huge cartels, a charismatic cult leader, a fascinating and ruthless woman, time travel, psychic powers, Nazis, androids, emigration to Mars, and mind-manipulating media and simulacra. Dick crowds more characters and more different points of view into the anarchic pages of this novel than in any of his other books. But it does not seem to go anywhere: it is a plunge into the deeper waters of Dick's universe, but without any clear reemergence into the air. The energy is more frenetic than transformative. Such a tour de force lacks the impact of Dick's major works, though it is a dazzling ride.

Despite all the plot elements that *The Simulacra* does contain, it lacks the idea of conceptual breakthrough from ordinary reality into a higher or altered state of consciousness. Without exception, Dick's major novels contain this theme, and in comparison a novel like this one seems a shade superficial. *The Simulacra* does carry the message that the way society appears to be structured is a complete fake, and that media manipulation conceals the real centers of power. But this exposure is not accompanied by any meaningful vision of transcendence.

The story takes place in Dick's standard near-future dystopia. The USEA (U.S. and Europe combined) is ruled by a single party in uneasy alliance with the giant cartels. The government is opposed by a fanatical cult, the Sons of Job, led by the elusive Bertold Goltz, who has access to a time-travel machine and who frequently materializes in the White House to harass the leaders. The country is nominally ruled by a First Lady, Nicole Thibodeaux, whose elderly husband ("der Alte") is replaced every four years. This matriarchal system is actually a cover for a ruling council, whom Nicole has never met. Nicole herself is just one of a succession of actresses taking the same name and playing the same part, and der Alte is a mere simulacrum. But as history is constantly being rewritten, the masses are kept in an unenlightened state by a steady diet of televised images of their beloved Nicole, a Magna Mater figure for the whole society. Only a select group at the top are privileged to know who really runs things.

The artists in the novel are as caught up in the general delusion as anyone else. Richard Kongrosian, the virtuoso psychokinetic pianist, is in love with Nicole. She is also idolized by Al Miller and Ian Duncan, who realize their dream of being invited to the White House to play their classical jugs. Their obsession is similar to Louis's with Pris in *We Can Build You*. When this kind of private delusion becomes a public article of faith, however, the whole society can be seen as schizophrenic, for the center about which it structures its universe is a complete fabrication: image without substance.

The character of Kongrosian combines features of both Hoppy and Bluthgeld from *Dr. Bloodmoney*. He is subject to paranoid delusions. He suffers from a phobic body odor caused he thinks by one of the insectlike Nitz commercials, which fly into people's homes and cars with their repellent messages. He also considers himself invisible and

the cause of all the accidents in the world. His psychokinetic power
goes out of control in the end, as his internal organs unexpectedly
change places with ordinary objects. He begins to play the part of the
variable element that warps and distorts other people's realities in unpredictable ways, but Dick fails to develop him fully in that role, as
he does, say, with Bluthgeld, or with Manfred in *Martian Time-Slip*
and Alys in *Flow My Tears, the Policeman Said.*

The characters in *The Simulacra* constantly seek escape from the
claustrophobic pressures of the world they live in, but none of the
available means offers much hope. Joining the Sons of Job is attractive
to many, but Bertold Goltz, its leader, is revealed in the end as the
head of the ruling council. Thus the government has co-opted the rev-
olution. Others seek out the last practicing psychiatrist, Dr. Egon Su-
perb, but he is not particularly effectual with Kongrosian, whose
perceptions are past adapting to the ersatz reality that surrounds him.

The favorite escape is emigration to Mars. Almost everyone in the
book at one time or another thinks of buying a minispaceship from a
"jalopy jungle"; these fly from place to place like roving used-car lots.
People are encouraged in this desire by papoolas, telepathic simulacra
of cute, furry little Martian creatures, which are used in the time-
honored sales technique of subliminal seduction. Innocent passersby
are ensnared with promises of freedom in a new world. But they tend
to take their need for illusion with them in the form of android
neighbors:

> A man, when he emigrated, could buy neighbors, buy the simulated pres-
> ence of life, the sound and motion of human activity—or at least its mechan-
> ical near-substitute—to bolster his morale in the new environment of
> unfamiliar stimuli and perhaps, god forbid, no stimuli at all. . . . The fam-
> nexdo were actually not next door at all; they were part of their owner's en-
> tourage. Communication with them was in essence a circular dialogue with
> oneself; the famnexdo, if they were functioning properly, picked up the covert
> hopes and dreams of the settler and detailed them back in an articulated fash-
> ion. Therapeutically, this was helpful, although from a cultural standpoint it
> was a trifle sterile. (chap. 5)

No one on Earth seems to know what the conditions are like on Mars:
it is enough that they are something different. The reality of other
worlds is typically deplorable in Dick: *The Three Stigmata of Palmer
Eldritch* and *Martian Time-Slip* portray the sterility of life in an alien

environment in some detail. Trading one fake reality for another proves to be no escape.

## *Now Wait for Last Year*

Although *Now Wait for Last Year* is usually grouped with the novels of Dick's late 1960s period, it was completed by late 1963, but it underwent revision before its first publication in 1966. Thus we may see it as the first of several novels in which drugs are a major element; the others are *The Three Stigmata of Palmer Eldritch, The Unteleported Man,* and *A Scanner Darkly.* In *Now Wait for Last Year* the drug in question, JJ-180, supposedly hallucinogenic, does more than alter consciousness: it takes the user backwards or forwards in time. It alters not just subjective reality, but also objective reality, and allows concourse between the parallel universes of different time tracks.

Dr. Eric Sweetscent is personal physician to Gino Molinari, UN Secretary and most powerful man in the world. Molinari is extraordinarily sensitive; he is more highly developed in the sense of sight, "the primary conduit linking the mind with external reality" (chap. 3). He sees deeply into people's souls with his penetrating eyes, burrowing beneath the surface of things like a "Mole"—his nickname. This ability causes him to fall sick constantly, however, as he empathetically manifests the physical symptoms of the diseases suffered by the people around him. His compulsion to be sick gives him an excuse not to fully implement the dictates of the inhuman humans from Lilistar, Earth's domineering ally in the war against an alien insectoid race called the reegs.

Kim Stanley Robinson has noted this war's parallel with Vietnam, which "makes our leaders the danger, and the alien enemy yet another victim of their aggression."[13] The reegs are good, generous, and peace-loving, as opposed to the Lilistarmen, who though human in form, are vicious. Lilistar's Prime Minister Frenesky's eyes, for example, are described as possessing "an attentiveness which made empathic understanding impossible; the eyes did not reflect any inner reality . . . they were a barrier that could not be penetrated this side of the tomb" (chap. 9). Appearances are deceiving: the alien embodies the divine, while the human disguises the demonic.

Molinari keeps himself in power as Earth's leader by bringing back other Molinaris from different time tracks, which he visits through JJ-

180, to take his place whenever he either dies of his empathetically acquired diseases or is assassinated. The public Molinari is a younger, more vital-looking simulacrum of himself, speaking lines programmed by a clever speechwriter. This deceptive use of media and image to enhance political power recalls *The Simulacra*. But there is a new element here: Molinari's quasi-Christlike nature (he takes on the suffering of others; he is "resurrected"). Dick based Molinari on Mussolini interpreted sympathetically;[14] he intensifies our ambivalence toward him by making him a kind of a savior. Because Molinari can perpetuate his power, Earth is finally able to extricate itself from its unwise involvement in the war against the reegs.

Eric Sweetscent, for his part, tries to create a desirable future for Earth by using JJ-180 to communicate with future versions of himself. At the same time he is trying to disentangle himself from his wife, who is hooked on the drug and has maliciously addicted him also. One acquaintance, observing them together, says, "Well, that's marriage these days. Legalized hate" (chap. 1). But try as he may, Eric cannot extricate himself emotionally from the relationship. He is both attracted and repelled. She is sexually perfect but hard-hearted. He imagines her body being turned into ice—breasts, hips, and buttocks—while the woman in her fades away.

After trying to escape from her and his own depression for the whole book, even to the point of nearly attempting suicide, he decides to take the advice of a robot taxicab:

To the cab he said suddenly, "If your wife were sick—"

"I have no wife, sir," the cab said. "Automatic Mechanisms never marry; everyone knows that."

"All right," Eric agreed. "If you were me, and your wife were sick, desperately so, with no hope of recovery, would you leave her? Or would you stay with her, even if you had traveled ten years into the future and knew for an absolute certainty that the damage to her brain could never be reversed? And staying with her would mean—"

"I can see what you mean, sir," the cab broke in. "It would mean no other life for you beyond caring for her."

"That's right," Eric said.

"I'd stay with her," the cab decided.

"Why?"

"Because," the cab said, "life is composed of reality configurations so constituted. To abandon her would be to say, I can't endure reality as such. I have to have uniquely special easier conditions."

"I think I agree," Eric said after a time. "I think I will stay with her."

"God bless you, sir," the cab said. "I can see that you're a good man." (chap. 14)

This conversation has been frequently cited by critics and is central to an understanding of Dick's worldview. The taxicab is right: there is no escape from the central problem of Eric's life. Reality has an element of fate that we must accept, although because there is an infinity of possible futures, it is not easy to tell what one's true fate is. Unlike Gino Molinari, Eric will not let another self live his life for him. He has looked ahead at a future self, one who divorced Kathy, and has decided to reject that possibility. This ending is hopeful because it suggests that man can live with his fate, and that is better than controlling it. In the tragic resolution lies his victory. He must find his *ground* in a bewildering array of parallel worlds and possible selves.

On one hand, then, we have the Molinari approach: he uses JJ-180 to break out of the fatality of history and linear time and borrow from other possible universes for the benefit of his own. On the other, we have Sweetscent, who is tempted by his vision of release through the drug from his unredeemed life in an imperfect would, but ultimately decides to play with the hand that has been dealt him. The love-hate relationship with his wife is an extension of his own lack of personal integration, and to turn his back on her would not solve that internal conflict. The reality-configuration, including the "bitch wife," is of his own creation. It is only he who can re-create it and redeem it.

## Clans of the Alphane Moon

Dick's next novel, *Clans of the Alphane Moon,* published in 1964, is one of his funniest. This is in spite of the fact that the plot centers around an even more lethal marital relationship than in *Now Wait for Last Year;* in *Clans* Chuck and Mary Rittersdorf are actually trying to kill each other. They follow the usual pattern: he is depressed and resigned in the midst of their breakup; she is bitchy and vindictive, planning to take him for all he is worth and more. Their showdown culminates out on the distant moon Alpha III M2, a former hospital world inhabited entirely by the clinically insane.

The former patients have adapted well to having been left alone by psychiatrists, living in relative peace with each other by grouping themselves in different "clans" according to their psychosis. Their social functions are also determined by their class of abnormality. The Pares (paranoids) live in Adolfville and constitute the statesman class. The Manses (manics), the warrior class, live in Da Vinci Heights. The Heebs (hebephrenics), the ascetic saints, inhabit Gandhitown. There are also the Skitzes (simple schizophrenics), Polys (polymorphic schizophrenics), Deps (depressives), and Ob-Coms (obsessive-compulsives). The Manses and Pares are the most powerful elements in the society, but all have their place, even the pitiful Heebs, who can hardly maintain themselves on a subsistence level but have psi powers and can work "miracles."

There is nothing inherently crazier about their society, in fact, than the one we find on Earth, where Chuck is caught up in a struggle between the CIA and a popular TV entertainer, Bunny Hentman. He innocently tries to work for both in order to make enough money to meet his wife's settlement demands, and succeeds only in making each side think he is betraying it to the opposition. His saving graces are Joan Trieste, a police psi who can save lives by causing time to back up before the time of death, and Lord Running Clam, a telepathic Ganymedean slime mold. Joan is the typical beautiful, younger woman who presents an empathic alternative to the horrid wife. Naturally Chuck has an affair with her. An asexual pile of yellow globes, Lord Running Clam is an unlikely embodiment of empathy: it saves Chuck from suicide, lines him up with Joan, and sacrifices its life to try to prevent his capture by an agent of Hentman.

Joan points out that Ganymedeans possess *caritas,* "the greatest of all the virtues." This most exalted quality is in short supply among Dick's human characters as a rule. However, Chuck and Mary, having spent their anger at the end, both forgive each other and decide to live together again (in their own settlement of "normals" on Alpha III M2). *Caritas* has touched their lives, in the case of Mary through a mystical vision produced by the Heeb saints.

"Normality" is, as Chuck declares, only a matter of degree. Everybody tends toward unbalance in one of the several directions indicated by the labeling of the Clans. The whole question of insanity, in fact, may be merely a function of whether one is on the inside or the outside. The novel suggests that people seek out those who share similar types of delusion and group themselves accordingly in tribes. It is an adaptation to the inescapable fact that reality is different in different states of consciousness, and no two people share the same reality. But such insularity is not necessarily good, for it tends to reinforce one's own brand of insanity. The chief Pare, Gabriel Baines, begins to see the limitations of his "solution" of constant suspicion about everyone else. When he saves the life of Annette, a Poly, he experiences for the first time in his life a moment of relief from the burden of being a Pare, of constantly keeping up his defenses.

At the end of the novel Chuck feels "the Paraclete," the Holy Spirit, entering his life when he realizes that he still loves Mary. This coincides with the moment that Lord Running Clam is resurrected from spores of its laser-blasted former self. The slime mold's amorphous form (it is fond of entering rooms by sliding under the door) makes it ideal as a bearer of the Holy Spirit. If humans could be metaphorically that fluid and flexible, and could flow through the barriers that they build between each other, they could live in true harmony—for the adaptive solution of the Clans is not a fully human deliverance.

## The Crack in Space

Although not published until 1966, *The Crack in Space* was completed in 1964 and logically stands next in the chronology. Its first seven chapters were published in *Fantasy and Science Fiction* as a short novel entitled "Cantata 140." In the expansion Dick completely reverses the drift of the original story.

In 2080 Jim Briskin is running for president, the first black man ever to do so. The most pressing social problem is overpopulation, and a hundred million people, mostly nonwhites, are suspended in deep-freeze waiting for better days. Briskin's campaign receives a boost when he advocates waking these "bibs" and sending them through a rent in the fabric of space-time, to emigrate into a virgin environment. At the end of "Cantata 140" this seems a real solution to the problem. In the full-length novel it becomes clear, as in other Dick novels such as *The Unteleported Man,* that emigration is not a solution but a catastrophe. For the new world is a parallel Earth inhabited by Sinanthropi, or Peking Men, who in the alternate reality have evolved along a different path than Homo sapiens, but are at least as intelligent. The crack between worlds thus becomes their opportunity to invade this Earth as well as ours to invade theirs.

The recurrence of the theme of the discovery of living ancient ancestors in modern times, as in *The Man Whose Teeth Were All Exactly Alike* and *The Simulacra,* suggests a symbolic incursion into modern consciousness of the buried, primitive self. The Peking Men are more advanced than we in certain respects, despite their stooped gait and sloping foreheads: they have built a flying machine propelled by the expansion of ice, and one of their elders has powers of telepathy and teleportation. But they are also innocents, easily mislead by George Walt, a mutant with two bodies and a single head, to believe that he is their fabled God of the Wind. When the elder discovers the ruse, he is disgusted at the deceitfulness and exploitative intentions of Homo sapiens. Indeed, except for Jim Briskin, there seem to be no human characters in the novel who are not mired down in petty, personal, materialistic concerns.

Despite flashes of the characteristic humor, *The Crack in Space* is substandard Dick. It relies on routine political intrigue and a meandering plot without compelling characters. It also lacks both the themes of the problematical marriage and the breakthrough to a higher reality that mark much of Dick's best work. A multifocal point of view is used, but without creating interesting contrasts. The subjective dimension is, in short, missing here in large degree.

## The Three Stigmata of Palmer Eldritch

Without a doubt one of Dick's finest novels, *The Three Stigmata of Palmer Eldritch* (published in 1965) has a powerful claim as his masterpiece. Certainly it qualifies as a breakthrough book, one about which Dick himself once commented, "It may be a unique book in the history of *writing—nothing* was ever done like this."[15] He may have been referring to the devastating way the novel suspends and ultimately destroys the reader's notions of objective reality.

Paul Williams has written of the novel's "out-of-control quality" as key to its greatness.[16] When, about fifty pages into the book, the characters start being exposed to the hallucinogenic drug Chew-Z, the reader is swept onto a wild ride that continues unabated through the end, absorbed in a quest for truth, and forced to ask, "What is really happening here? What is real and what is hallucination?" In finding an answer, one must grapple with some puzzling, disturbing, and profound philosophical questions.

The setting is a future Earth where the environment has heated up intolerably: 180-degree weather in New York, portable cooling units, resorts in Antarctica. Because of overpopulation, people are "drafted" to emigrate to the even more miserable environments of Mars and other planets. Barney Mayerson carries around a portable computer psychiatrist, Dr. Smile, to help him become insane enough to avoid the draft. Barney is a "pre-fash," a recognitive fashion consultant, at a company that makes "layouts," or miniaturized ideal worlds replete with all the accessories of modern life. The colonists, to escape the dreary reality of their hovels, take a hallucinogenic drug, Can-D. It enables them to fuse their minds together and enter the world of the "layout," to revel fleetingly in the bodies of the doll-figures of glamorous Perky Pat and her boyfriend Walt—dressing fashionably, driving in sports cars, going to the beach, having sex. Barney eventually ends up on Mars himself, taking the drug and participating in this escapist idyll of eternal youth and pleasure.

The colonists have something of a theological debate going to the reality of the Can-D experience. Some regard the drug-induced "translation" of the artificial layout into a concrete experience of Earth as an actual transubstantiation of the profane into the holy. Others regard the change as one of appearances only, not of essence. Fran Schein sees it as an authentic spiritual experience of dying to the corporeal body and entering an immortal body; to Sam Regan, it is a consummation of the senses. Sam chews Can-D not to be free from sin, as does Fran, but to be free to act out desires that lie outside normal social boundaries: "While translated one could commit incest, murder, anything, and it remained from a juridical standpoint a mere fantasy, an impotent wish only" (chap. 3). However, the Perky Pat layouts, rather than encouraging the indulgence of such antisocial impulses, conventionalize and trivialize the Can-D trippers' plunge into absolute freedom. While translated, Sam is content to focus on snatching a few minutes of extramarital sexual pleasure with Fran.

The users of psychedelic drugs in the 1960s had similarly varying interpretations of the meaning of the acid trip. Spiritual and hedonistic motives were frequently mixed. But it should be remembered that Dick completed *Three Stigmata* in 1964, long before the heyday of LSD or before attempts of Timothy Leary and others to legitimize the drug experience by touting it as the basis of all true religion.

Everything connected with the drugs in the novel has religious overtones. The Perky Pat layout is likened to the lost Eden; the inhospitable desert of Mars becomes the colonists' "promised land" (chap. 9). Barney must "atone" for the sin that has brought him to Mars. Religious fanatic Anne Hawthorne, who becomes Barney's lover, transfers her faith in God to faith in immortality through the drug.

An important adjunct to the use of drugs in the novels in another artificial means of changing consciousness called E Therapy. A mad scientist type, Dr. Denkmal (think bad?), stimulates a gland causing the frontal lobe to expand. All the richest people in society pursue his expensive treatment and develop "bubbleheads," which give them a fashionably hydrocephalic appearance, and their skins become horny rinds. Although the process is supposed to uplift one mentally and spiritually, Leo Bulero, Barney's boss, does not seem particularly "evolved," even though he feels he is becoming a superior type of human. Also, the therapy does not always take, as in the case of Barney's ex-wife Emily, who devolves. Like Can-D, E Therapy produces a false escape from the limitations of ordinary reality. What is particularly amusing is how E Therapy's monstrous side effects are embraced by society as chic.

Palmer Eldritch is a negative messiah in the novel, back from a lengthy interplanetary quest with a new drug, Chew-Z, and the message that it, unlike Can-D, truly allows the user to fulfill all his desires. He claims it produces no fantasy state, but a "genuine new universe" (chap. 6). Furthermore, it requires no layout, or artificial setting, for the experience. It gives one the power to create any reality and materialize anything one wishes—but at a cost, for Palmer Eldritch then becomes the evil god of one's hallucinated world. The materialization of one's desires tends to turn ghastly. At any time, the people in one's Chew-Z fantasy may reveal themselves as bearing Eldritch's "stigmata"—his artificial hand, slitted mechanical eyes, and steel teeth—even after the drug's effects have seemingly worn off. The tendency of people to change into Eldritch is a metaphor for the danger of evolutionary reversion to the unfeeling and mechanical. The pollution of the world by these images of the stigmata easily spreads even to those who have not taken the drug, throwing into doubt the substantiality of everybody's reality. Barney is turned into a phantom in a future world that regards him as only semi-real, and then finds himself changing into Eldritch. Thus Chew-Z, promising the fulfillment of all desires, only produces a nightmare from which one perhaps never awakes.

The novel's unlikely hero, Leo Bulero, Barney's boss, is reminiscent of Arnie Kott in *Martian Time-Slip*—a crass, selfish, materialistic businessman, but nonetheless a sympathetic character. He is the relatively good human who opposes the evil deity—for Palmer Eldritch is more than a man: he has become possessed by an alien creature with vast powers. On a couple of occasions Dick pointed to the opening epigraph of the novel, a quotation from an interoffice memo by Leo Bulero, as having central thematic significance: "I mean, after all; you have to consider we're only made out of dust. That's admittedly not much to go on and we shouldn't forget that. But even considering, it's a sort of bad beginning, we're not doing too bad. So I personally have faith that even in this lousy situation we're faced with we can make it. You get me?" To really *know* we are only made of dust, the entire world as we perceive it must be revealed as maya, as illusion. This happens to both Leo and Barney when through Chew-Z they are pulled into Palmer Eldritch's universe, which although it resembles their own, is alien and evil at its heart. In a reversal of Christ's sacrifice, the communicant takes on the evil god's stigmata and undergoes a spiritual death so that the ghoulish thing that is Eldritch may perpetuate itself. Eldritch switches bodies with Barney so when Leo tries to kill him, Barney will die instead.

The distortions of reality represented by Eldritch's three stigmata— artificial hand, eyes, and teeth-correspond to "the evil, negative trinity of alienation, blurred reality, and despair" (chap. 13). Leo realizes these are "accidents" or surface appearances: the essence is within him, an absolute that Eldritch cannot reach. Or can he? At the end Leo makes a slip: consumed with his Faustian desire for evolution through E Therapy into a superior human form, he momentarily forgets his own identity and believes he is Palmer Eldritch. He is inflated, like the bubblehead he is, with the notion of being the "Protector" of the human race—an ersatz godhead. Eldritch is subtly undermining him because relatively good as he is, he has still eaten the apple and is not yet liberated from the bondage of original sin. Barney's solution, to stay on Mars and cultivate his garden à la Candide, is finally more humane and dignified than Leo's inflated-hero complex.

In a sense, drugs are a red herring in *Three Stigmata*. Altered states of consciousness exist in other Dick novels without depending on artificial means. Can-D and Chew-Z are, rather, pretexts for revealing the transiency of the fabric of reality woven by our perceptions and conditioning. The questions remain: Is the essence one of unmitigated evil? Do we embrace maya because reality is too hideous to face? The answer for Dick is clearly no—although this is a conclusion one draws from looking at the gnosticism that underlies the entire body of his work from start to finish and that became explicit in *VALIS*.

The Gnostic religion, which flourished in the first through third centuries A.D., provides an excellent paradigm for understanding the type of religious awareness that much science fiction favors. The Gnostics, regarded as heretics by the faction that became orthodox Christianity, were radical transcendentalists. They believed that man is essentially pure spirit (pneuma), trapped in a cage of flesh. The world cannot be taken at face value: it is one vast snare for the senses, causing man to forget his inner spiritual reality. The being who created it was not God: it was a lower power, an "archon" or demiurge, who masquerades as God to the unsuspecting. This creator is not good but evil, or at least ignorant and self-deluded. Mankind's goal must be to transcend its own nescience through gnosis. Gnostic sects had their own subjective science to accomplish this, involving the development of mental powers to break the tyranny of the archons, and the realization of human pneuma as identical with the divine spirit of God.

The Gnostic God's reality as pure Being recalls Hindu and Buddhist notions of the Absolute that underlies and permeates all relative existence. Gnostics believed that rather than being inherently sinful or fallen, the divine pneumatic essence of man has the capability to transcend the flesh and the material world ruled by the demiurge, and merge with the true God.

The Gnostic, who seeks liberation rather than salvation, pays no allegiance to the demiurge. Having created man imprisoned and ignorant, the demiurge tries to make sure he stays that way. To the Gnostic who rebels against his ignominious lot, the demiurge is a cosmic Big Brother, always watching malevolently and voyeuristically. In *Eye in the Sky* the hateful giant eye perched in the highest heaven is a potent image of this evil super-being. Palmer Eldritch is another: Barney sees him as something "ugly and foreign that entered one of our race like an ailment," an entity whose knowledge derived from "unending solitary brooding" in the vastness of interstellar space (chap. 12). It is an open question in the novel as to whether Eldritch has not indeed been possessed by *the* God. This question as to whether God is actually evil will also arise in the powerful short story "Faith of Our Fathers." However, it will not be resolved until *VALIS* and the other novels from Dick's later years.

Certainly Palmer Eldritch is not omnipotent and suffers under some of the same limitations as do mere mortals. He is destined to be slain by Leo Bulero. He tries to help Barney overcome his emotional dependency on Emily. Barney reflects: "Should I tell you how it tried to help me, in its own way? And yet—how fettered it was, too, by the forces of fate, which seem to transcend all that live, including it as much as ourselves" (chap. 12). Anne Hawthorne gives a Gnostic corrective to Barney's feeling that Eldritch is God:

"Don't tell us, Barney, that whatever entered Palmer Eldritch *is* God, because you don't know that much about Him; no one can. But that living entity from intersystem space may, like us, be shaped in His image. A way He selected of showing Himself to us. If the map is not the territory, *the pot is not the potter.* So don't talk ontology, Barney; don't say *is.*" (chap. 13)

It is hard enough to judge reality in the phenomenal world; the lesson Dick drives home time and again is that our realities are built on the flimsiest of structures, which a sudden change of consciousness will topple. How much harder, then, to know the nature of God?

But whatever forces, psychological or cosmic, are responsible for the maya of existence, they cannot be ultimate ones. Absolute power in the field of illusion does not translate to omnipotence. Dick makes that clear enough in *The Three Stigmata of Palmer Eldritch.* It is not merely a novel about the pervasiveness of evil, but about humans' possibilities of transcending even the most powerful adversary.

## The Zap Gun

*The Zap Gun* was written in 1964, more or less concurrently with *The Penultimate Truth,* and is one of several of Dick's good second-rank novels of the 1960s that tends to be overlooked. One reason for this may be the trashy title, which resulted because the book was written to order for the paperback house, Pyramid Books, who wanted to publish two novels called *The Zap Gun* and *Space Opera,* the latter title being assigned to Jack Vance. These titles may have had something to do with self-parody of the genre, but Dick's novel had very little to do with its title, either in content or in spirit. Although highly humorous, its comedy does not derive from parody of hackneyed science-fiction formulas, but rather from satire on the arms race and techniques of political manipulation.

At the basis of Dick's political satire is a challenge to the very notion of consensual reality, which is a product of mass consciousness, a lowest common denominator of belief that the media, moneyed interests, and the government conspire to perpetuate. Thus in *The Zap Gun* we have a whole society of "pursaps" (pure saps) convinced that bigger and better wonder weapons are continually being built, while only the "cogs" (the knowledgeable elite) know the truth: that the new wonder weapons are nonfunctional and work only in filmed simulations. The weapons are "plowshared"—converted to peaceful uses, like swords beaten to plowshares. For example, a guidance system is plowshared as a ceramic owl to hold cigars and pencils. Both major powers have agreed on plowsharing as a safe way of conducting an arms race and thus keeping the pursaps happy.

Lars Powderdry is a "weapons fashion designer" who goes into drug-induced mediumistic trances to meet the consumer demand for new weapons concepts. One of his own designs, plowshared into a super-computer in the shape of a head named "Ol' Orville," can answer virtually any question and analyzes Lars himself, diagnosing his psychological state as "Waffenlos"—weaponless, like Parsifal, whose name means "pure fool." Lars is no better off, really, than the pursaps, for none of his weapons actually works. And he even harbors a near-castration fear of losing his psychic talent, such as it is. He may have cog status, but it does very little to make his life meaningful.

When a real threat to Earth's security manifests in the form of alien satellites, Lars and his counterpart from the Eastern bloc, Lilo Topchev, are forced to pool their talents. Together they search in the hyperdimensional "Other World" that they contact during their trance states for a real weapon that will work against the invaders. Ironically, in the process they discover that their cognitions are picked up not from some mystic repository of archetypes but from the mind of a mad comic book artist, Oral Giacomini, creator of *The Blue Cephalopod Man from Titan.* Perhaps Dick's implication is that the forces that shape our world can be found in trash—in novels with names like *The Zap Gun,* for instance. If the reality of this novel has been warped by the fantasies of an Oral Giacomini, is it out of the question that a Philip K. Dick could affect ours? Perhaps the visions of the inspired and the obsessed slip into the collective psyche, to emerge in various manifestations of societal behavior, such as the weapons a country chooses to build.

In *The Zap Gun* a character named Surley G. Febbs represents the lowest common denominator of average man, a crackpot like Jack Isidore but without any redeeming qualities. He is discovered by a computer to have tastes and opinions that are ideally average. This distinction qualifies him to be a "concomody," one of only six people in the country who will advise the government on how new weapons designs should be plowshared. Being a pursap, Febbs believes everything he is told in the media and assumes the weapons are real; the perpetuation of the Cold War economy depends on this myth. Like many know-nothings in real life, Febbs magnifies his ignorance with egoism and pride, as when he obliterates his own followers, his fellow concomodies with a zap gun (the sole appearance of the title weapon in the novel). Febbs's downfall is an empathy game that he is tricked into playing; it causes him to identify telepathically with the plight of a lost creature in a maze, and he becomes lost in permanent psychosis. Since his ideas had been exclusively defined by the consensus, the shock of having to think as an individual and experience the *idios kosmos* completely blasts his unstable reality.

In contrast, Lars is able to play the empathy game without losing his mind, for he is introspective, like all Dick's heroes, albeit morbidly so. He plays out his inner conflicts on the field of male-female relationships, which are always for Dick of as much importance as any of his science-fictional concerns. Lilo is beautiful and deadly (she tries to poison Lars at their first meeting). Nevertheless, Lars is irresistibly attracted to her, to the point of giving up his mistress, Maren Faine, a similarly destructive anima type of woman who threatens them both with a gun but ends up turning it on herself. Toward the end of the novel Lars finds himself in a suicidal depression, but Ol' Orville, who proves to be a wise machine in the tradition of the talking taxi in *Now Wait for Last Year,* counsels him to have sex with Lilo instead of killing himself. They take the advice, and at last seem to have worked out an adequate rapprochement between the ever-warring sexes, who are much more serious opponents in this book than the subtly collusive East and West.

## The Penultimate Truth

As in *The Zap Gun,* Dick posits a ruling elite and a massive underclass in *The Penultimate Truth* (1964). This novel focuses on the theme of fakery and its uses in structuring political realities. A major hoax is perpetrated against most of the Earth's population, which retreats underground in huge "ant tanks" to avoid being killed in a nuclear war. The war ends, but the leaders choose not to tell these "tankers." The tankers are kept busy manufacturing robots called "leadies" while being fed television images of the war that is supposedly raging above, fought by the leadies. The elite, the "Yance-men," are glorified speechwriters who program a folksy politician simulacrum named Yancy to pacify the tankers with propaganda. Meanwhile, the Yance-men have the Earth to themselves, living like medieval robber barons on huge private "demesnes." Most of the novel is concerned with the power struggle between Stanton Brose, the aged and grossly fat top dog among Yance-men, and David Lantano, a Cherokee Indian from six centuries in the past.

The plot of the novel is cobbled together from diverse elements of three of Dick's short stories, "The Defenders," "The Unreconstructed M," and "The Mold of Yancy," with ideas from *Dr. Futurity* and *The Man Whose Teeth Were All Exactly Alike* thrown in for good measure. All these elements, however, have been elaborated with plenty of extra twists, and the resulting grab bag of complicated narrative strands contains plenty of loose ends. *The Penultimate Truth* is not one of Dick's better novels, and it lacks the character interest and outrageous humor of *The Zap Gun.* But it is well worth reading as a key work in Dick's effort to deconstruct reality and to ask the question: how do we decide what is true?

The tankers are like the pursaps. Basically, they want to be misled; they cannot accept the truth. And the leaders give them what they want: the illusion that war is necessary and inevitable. Like the dwellers in Plato's cave, the tankers are hypnotized by images on the wall, which, to them, *are* the reality. They forget the past so quickly that documentary filmmakers can get away with major oversights and inconsistencies in their attempts to rewrite history. Even when Lantano gains power at the end and declares the war over, he does not tell the tankers that they have been deceived all along. And despite the tanker Nicholas St. James's resolve to disseminate the truth about the Yancemen's great deception, there is no guarantee that people will not stay buried in ignorance even when they come up to the surface. When they emerge from their ant tanks, they may well bring war back with them. It was not the humans, in fact, who had done away with it. The reasonable leadies had originated the idea that saying you were fighting was just as good as really doing it; for as long as people believed the lie, why waste the resources in actual warfare?

Dick delights in devising paradoxes to illustrate the idea that getting to the ultimate truth is practically impossible. There is always another layer to be penetrated: every new truth turns out to be penultimate. For example, Lantano tries to convince another Yance-man, Joseph Adams, that Brose has committed "the ultimate in fakery" by having a "Gestalt-macher," a fiendishly clever killing machine, murder one of his own men, and leave clues to cast suspicion on himself. Since clues left by a macher would logically be spurious, left only to frame a human being, Brose would have to be considered innocent. But Brose is guilty because he programmed the macher: so says Lantano. This ingenious explanation, however, is merely the penultimate truth, since Lantano is the real killer and is trying to motivate Adams to kill Brose. He misleads Adams in order to rid Earth of a tyrant.

Lantano is a kind messiah figure: he is immortal, continually regenerating himself through manipulations with time travel. In that respect he is somewhat reminiscent of Gino Molinari in *Now Wait for Last Year,* although he is not as well developed as a character. He has the best interests of the tankers at heart, and aims to release them from this oppression and to lift the veil of lies. He slays the dragon Brose. He is charismatic, eloquent, empathetic, but he looks like Yancy the simulacrum that people have trusted because they needed a father figure to believe in. Perhaps he can keep the peace, if in the new era of his leadership they simply continue to project their idealizations on his televised image in their need to be told what to think. But it will be at the expense of the truth. And if the masses are not led out of ignorance, no peace will be good enough.

The typical Philip K. Dick novel is a paradigm of reality deconstruction; and *The Penultimate Truth* in its somewhat ill-structured way, with all its improbabilities and looseness, is honest in its headlong plunge through its willful convolutions of plot. Since it is not offering any ultimate truth, after all, it hardly need disguise itself in perfect form.

## Chapter Five
# The Late Sixties

*The Unteleported Man (Lies, Inc.)*

Dick's novels of the late 1960s move into more subjective realms than most of those discussed to this point, with the exception of *Martian Time-Slip* and *The Three Stigmata of Palmer Eldritch*. Theological, phenomenological, and ontological questions come to the forefront; the political themes of such novels as *The Penultimate Truth* recede to the background, although it might be said that politics is subsumed in larger philosophical concerns about the nature of reality. *The Unteleported Man* is a transitional work; in fact, Dick moves into radically different territory midway through the book, so that it seems like two very different works rather arbitrarily patched together.

The first half of this novel was originally published in *Fantastic* in December 1964. Ace Books was to publish an expanded version, but when Dick sent them the second half (evidently written in early 1965), it turned out to be the most bizarre and confusing piece of writing he ever produced, before or since. It had only a tenuous relationship with what had gone before in the story, and Donald A. Wollheim, the Ace editor, rejected it. Instead, in 1966 he published the first half as complete in itself, as part of one of the Ace Double Novel series.

The second half was resurrected for the 1983 Berkley reprinting of the complete, "uncensored" version of *The Unteleported Man.* That version is marred by three gaps in the second half where manuscript pages had been lost.

After the Berkley version was published, a revised manuscript turned up among Dick's papers, with some rewritten scenes in the first half and a repositioning of the second half at a point about two thirds of the way through the first half. Two of the gaps still remained; the section in which the third gap appeared was dropped in the revision. This third version of the book was published by Victor Gollancz in 1984 under Dick's new title of *Lies, Inc.,* the gaps being filled creatively with passages written by John Sladek. Then, in 1985, the missing manuscript pages were found and published separately in *Philip K. Dick Society Newsletter.*[1]

The first half of *The Unteleported Man* is fairly routine early-1960s Dick, a political intrigue set in a world where much of Earth's population is emigrating via teleportation to a distant planet, Whale's Mouth. Rachmael ben Applebaum believes that conditions there are not as idyllic as they are painted in the television ads of Trails of Hoffman Limited, which controls the teleportation equipment and Whale's Mouth. Rather than teleport there instantaneously, he prefers to fly in his ship, the *Omphalos,* a voyage that will take eighteen years. Lies, Inc., a private intelligence organization, takes an interest in his quixotic project; and with their suspicions aroused about Whale's Mouth, they decide to invade. There they find a military dictatorship, a garrison state modeled after Sparta. The first half ends with the battle still raging.

The second half of the story does not resolve the battle; it begins as Rachmael, who has decided after all to teleport to Whale's Mouth, is shot by an LSD dart. This sets off a series of psychedelic experiences involving a number of "paraworlds," or different classes of hallucinated worlds experienced in altered states of consciousness. In one of these Rachmael encounters a grotesque, alien, one-eyed creature that has apparently taken over the mind of the archvillain, Theodoric Ferry, head of Trails of Hoffman Limited, in a manner recalling the possession of Palmer Eldritch by the alien super-being. As Rachmael and Freya, whom he loves, stumble separately through a series of paraworlds, it is hard to say whether they or the reader is more disoriented.

The second half culminates in Rachmael's traveling back in time to before he teleported. Thus in a sense he remains "unteleported," as if the second half of the book never happened. The rewritten ending of *Lies, Inc.* changes the story somewhat, as it has him about to teleport back to Whale's Mouth, for all we know to repeat the cycle indefinitely. All of Dick's revisions in *Lies, Inc.,* in fact, heighten the complexity of an already impenetrable fiction.

Neither the Berkley nor the Gollancz version of the novel solves the inherent problem of the two disparate texts. Both halves deal with the problem of determining reality: the first half is about a giant political hoax reminiscent of *The Penultimate Truth* or *The Simulacra,* and the second half is about attempts to generate paraworlds of perceptual delusion. But stylistically it is like trying to marry the first half of *The Crack in Space* to the last half of *The Three Stigmata of Palmer Eldritch.*

It doesn't work. Yet the end result still fascinates—primarily because the material of the second half is so out of both the author's and the reader's control that the sense of objective reality dissolves altogether. We are immersed in total insanity. And because the structure of the novel is so unsatisfactory, there is no transcendent artistry to tie things together and reassure us.

One of the interesting elements in the second half of the novel is the appearance of a text by a Dr. Bloode that seems to describe in detail both the past and future of the main characters. However, it is constantly coming out in new "editions," as fluid and specific as life itself. At one point it almost traps Theodoric Ferry in the mind-warping experience of reading about the moment in which he is reading about himself reading . . . one of those paradoxes (like the one that brought down Surley G. Febbs in *The Zap Gun*) to which the power-inflated, unreflective, unempathetic consciousness is especially susceptible.

Since at several points characters read verbatim descriptions of events that will happen to them later in the book, Dr. Bloode's text is, essentially, *The Unteleported Man.* Thus Dick's book makes an appearance in his own novel—as a *character,* since Dr. Bloode's text turns out to be a life form, a "Ganymede life mirror" that reflects a person's thoughts back to him. This text is the ultimate lie, in that it purports to describe reality as it happens and will happen, ignoring the fact that other mutually exclusive editions of the text are constantly contradicting and replacing each other. In Dick's multiverse, the acts of observation and description are hopelessly complex.

Ironically, it is only in a paraworld outside the text of the novel as it exists in any of its three published versions that Dick shows the way out of the maze he has constructed. In the rediscovered pages filling the gap eliminated by Dick in the *Lies, Inc.* revision, Rachmael has a sudden insight about the true nature of the Dr. Bloode text: "Not everything which he read in the Dr. Bloode text was true. . . . Simply because it was written down—that in no sense made it binding, on him or on anyone else. It could become valid—if he let it. But the choice; that remained totally with him . . . and with the other humans involved. For better or worse."[2]

## Counter-Clock World

*Counter-Clock World* comes next in the sequence, the beginning of a period in which, according to Dick, "I had a different marriage, different child, different house, different community, and was writing less and having more trouble."[3] Perhaps because a struggle with writer's block was slowing his pace, this novel has a more serious and darker tone than most of his earlier ones.

Its premise is that, due to something called the Hobart Phase, time has started to run backwards. Dead people come back to life in their graves; living people grow continually younger until they reenter their mothers' wombs. Food is regurgitated in its original form, and while eating is considered obscene, waste ("sogum") is "imbibed" through tubes in public. People say "goodbye" when they greet each other, "hello" when they part. The Library, instead of preserving knowledge, has the purpose of eradicating it and has become a bureaucracy with immense power.

Critics have derided Dick's use of time reversal as completely illogical and inconsistent, for not everything is reversed—people still talk and act in forward linear fashion—but of course they would, from their frame of reference, and it is from their perspective, not ours, that the story is told. The principle of causality is not overturned; it is just that effects precede the causes.

Sebastian Hermes, the owner of a "vitarium," which resurrects awaking "deaders," discovers the location of the grave of the Anarch Peak, founder of the Udi cult, and resurrects him. Peak was a black spiritual leader of true dignity and vision, but his ideas have been distorted and institutionalized by his followers. Current Udi leader, Ray Roberts, has made it, in the honorable tradition of many religions, into a militant political organization with terrorist elements. Sebastian is caught in the struggle between the Uditi and the Library to take possession of Peak.

Lotta, Sebastian's wife, is a meek, inept, dependent type whom he thoughtlessly sends to the Library to do research on Roberts. She is detained and interrogated on Peak's whereabouts. Officer Joe Tinbane, who is in love with her, shoots his way in and rescues her. In the meantime, Sebastian has been easily seduced by Ann Fisher, a Library undercover agent. She is everything Lotta is not: sexually aggressive, dangerous, ruthless, and dominating. Ann causes him to lose Peak, orders Tinbane's death, and vows to kill Sebastian himself. At first, she is as evil an anima figure as any to be found in Dick. Understandably, Sebastian determines to kill her, but after seeing a vision of the Anarch who informs him that he is in love with Ann, he saves her life by warning her of Udi assassins.

Thus Dick's hero takes an important psychological step: rather than trying to destroy his anima, he makes his peace with her. It is an integrative, evolutionary development that shows increasing maturity and depth in Dick's male characters. One cannot kill one's projection on other persons by killing them. By not giving in to vengeance, Sebastian preserves the possibility of withdrawing his anima projection from Ann Fisher. At the same time, she becomes a slightly more sympathetic character for the reader. Sebastian redeems himself with Lotta by rescuing her from the Library. They forgive each other, but all is not well: the evil of the world is still abroad, and Lotta, embodying the ever-vulnerable good, is killed by one of Roberts's men. Still, the darkness within Sebastian's soul has been expiated somewhat.

In a 1981 letter describing *The Owl in Daylight,* the novel he was working on at the time he died, Dick discusses how he has adapted the structure of Dante's *Commedia*:

*Inferno* is characterized by metal, by repetition, total karmic control, total recycling of everything forever, as if time has stopped. In *Purgatorio*—get this!—*time runs backward.* And there is some freedom. This is a realm that partakes half of *Inferno* and half of *Paradiso*; it is a mixture. The mode is walking. Some change exists. Karma has power but can be broken by the right acts. . . . When you perform the right act, instantly the karmic fetters loosen [*Paradiso*]. The colors lighten. Brightness enters. The mode is flying, not walking. Time flows forward; there is constant redemption.[4]

With hindsight, then, we can say that *Counter-Clock World,* with its metaphor of time reversal, is purgatorial. Despite the slaughter of two out of its three main characters, it is a hopeful book. Sebastian makes the right choices at the end, and the impersonal bonds of fate or karma, represented by the Church (the Udi cult) and State (the Library) begin to loosen. With prophetic perceptivity, he hears the deaders below the ground beginning to awake all at once, a clear implication that apocalypse—in the sense of divine revelation—is at hand. Time is ready to start flowing forward.

As a counterpoint to the narrative itself, which is full of the frailty of life and love in the face of monolithic external forces, each chapter in *Counter-Clock World* begins with a quotation about the nature of God, time, or eternity from such writers as St. Augustine, Erigena, and Boethius. Their presence changes the effect of the novel by giving it a transcendent context of timeless truth. The Anarch Peak, having risen from the dead, discovers the validity of these visionaries as if for the first time. With his Lucretian philosophy that although lives die, life lives on, Peak affirms an immutable state of being underlying transient forms. As David Hartwell has pointed out, Dick is here attempting to integrate religious and metaphysical thought from Epicureanism through prominent Christian philosophers.[5] *Counter-Clock World* is an ambitious novel, underread and underrated in the Dick canon.

## *The Ganymede Takeover*

A minor effort of this period, *The Ganymede Takeover* was written in collaboration with Ray Nelson and published by Ace Books in 1967. Although in an interview Dick said, "He wrote the book and I just spruced it up for sale," by Nelson's account it was a more equal collaboration.[6] Both Dick and Nelson wrote outlines, and traded parts back and forth during the actual writing. Dick did the final draft. As Kim Stanley Robinson points out, it is derivative of *The Game-Players of Titan* (a much better novel), with the situation of evil telepathic aliens who have conquered Earth.[7]

In *The Ganymede Takeover* the aliens are large worms, who despite their form have a weakness for human culture: one collects model airplanes, another named Mekkis develops an obsession with the work of psychologist Dr. Rudolph Balkani. Balkani's "oblivion therapy" involves sensory deprivation treatment and makes a schizophrenic of the chief female character, Joan Hiashi. It also short-circuits the Ganymedian Great Common to which Mekkis is connected mentally. The reason for this devastating effect seems to be that the Nothingness at the basis of reality is too much for any mind, human or alien, to bear. Balkani himself commits suicide after smashing a robot simulacrum of Joan Hiashi, which of course cannot return his love. Oblivion therapy is a parody (and anticipation) of psychological techniques that break down the subject's ego, supposedly for his benefit. The effect on the real Joan Hiashi, however, is to turn her into a living robot whose pseudomystical state of nirvana is exposed as psychosis when she reveals her disgust with humanity: "we are all monsters . . . demons from hell—foul, filthy, perverted and evil" (chap. 8).

To Mekkis, Balkani's theories are "the ultimate truth of existence" (chap. 13). When Balkani dies, he takes on Balkani's identity and continues his work, plunging into a seductive solipsism. Mekkis thinks that because mind structures reality, reality is completely subjective, so that he doesn't need to worry about his enemies. Dick's own position is more subtle: although through our consciousness we partially create the world we inhabit, we also live in the world created by other consciousnesses. Reality is thus an interference pattern of interpenetrating subjectivities. We can never be complacent about what reality is because consciousnesses we are unconscious of may be shaping it for us.

Peace and happiness are ironically identified in the novel as synonymous with the oblivion of Pure Nothingness. Joan Hiashi, merging into unified consciousness in the isolation tank, loses her sense of ego and personality. Thus, although Balkani is right, "the greatest happiness possible for a human being" existed in that Absolute, "Unfortunately, no one remained to enjoy it" (chap. 7). Here there seems to be an unease with the prospect of pure transcendence, as with the telepathic joining of minds in a group consciousness. In either case, Dick is reluctant to let go of the principle of the individual consciousness, in its uniqueness, dignity, and relative freedom. He seeks an integrated solution to the problem of resolving two opposites: the evolutionary imperative to develop higher states of consciousness, and the inertia of the individual life with its freight of memory and fatality. Not until the late novels will this integration be completely achieved.

## *Do Androids Dream of Electric Sheep?*

Most critics agree that Dick's next novel was one of his best: *Do Androids Dream of Electric Sheep?* It was completed in 1966 and published in hardcover by Doubleday in 1968. In 1982, it was made into the film, *Blade Runner,* directed by Ridley Scott. Despite its originality and its striking, evocative visuals, the film plucks elements of the novel out of their context, making them somewhat less intelligible and less radical than in the original. Additionally, Dick's humor and his metaphysics are missing from the movie. However, when the novel was reissued in paperback as *Blade Runner* in 1982, it became Dick's all-time best-seller and no doubt introduced him to many readers.

Perhaps in no other novel did Dick grapple as boldly with the question "What does it mean to be human?" The reader is continually challenged to evaluate how human the androids are and how mechanical the humans are. The androids are not mere machines like most of the simulacra in Dick's other novels: they are artificial people made from organic materials; they have free will and emotions like fear and love. Physically and behaviorally they are indistinguishable from real people. They can even believe themselves to be human because of implanted artificial memory tapes. The one thing they seem to lack is empathy—the ability to identify with the sufferings and joys of other life forms. On the other hand, the empathic ability of various human characters is also frequently called into question.

Rick Deckard is a bounty hunter whose job it is to hunt down and kill escaped androids. He can distinguish androids from humans by giving them an empathy test to determine if they have the appropriate feelings about the death of animals; any indifference brands one as an android. In this postnuclear war society animals have become mostly extinct, and the world is slowly dying from the radioactive dust. Thus, almost obsessive value has been placed on the living animals that remain, and owning one or more has become a status symbol. For those unable to afford the exorbitant prices, a whole industry has arisen to sell cleverly designed electric animals, nearly indistinguishable from real ones. Deckard and his wife, for instance, possess an electric sheep that grazes on the roof of their conapt building.

The Deckards, a typical couple, live a thoroughly artificial life centered upon a "Penfield machine" that provides artificial brain stimulation inducing a variety of moods, from "awareness of the manifold possibilities open to me in the future" to a "six-hour self-accusatory depression" (chap. 1). The novel begins with a brilliant scene where he is trying to convince her to dial a setting on the machine that will put her in a mood to dial—although, as she points out, if she doesn't want to dial, the desire to dial would be the last thing she would want to dial.

Like everyone else, the Deckards follow the religion of Mercerism, which is a mechanized substitute for real human contact. By squeezing the handles of a Mercer box, one can fuse one's consciousness with that of everyone else, and empathetically participate in the sufferings of a TV messiah figure named Wilbur Mercer. Mercer is continually ascending a steep hill while being stoned by anonymous killers—and when he is hit, all those in contact with him actually bleed.

Late in the book Mercer is exposed as a hoax, an actor on a stage set—yet somehow despite its artificial trappings the religion works. Mercer can materialize to help those who believe in him, as he does in the case of both Deckard and John Isidore, a mentally retarded "chick-

enhead" who is the book's most empathic character. Mercer is a kind
of benevolent Palmer Eldritch, who can enter the worlds of Mercerites
and give them the benefit of his mercy. Only on the level of "accidents"—or appearances—is he a fraud. Though artificially contrived,
the religion bestows a real experience of empathy. In the same way, the
androids, though superficially artificial, have life and humanity—to a
point. There is something a bit chilly about them, like "a breath from
the vacuum between inhabited worlds, in fact from nowhere" (chap.
6).

In order to get the money to realize his dreams to acquire a living
animal, Deckard must fulfill his assignment to kill a group of six androids of a particularly advanced and dangerous type. As he does so,
he realizes he is developing empathy for them, which Dick encourages
in the reader as well by referring to them as "he" and "she," never "it."
Deckard finds himself sexually attracted to an android named Rachael
Rosen. With her childlike, somewhat androgynous body, but with the
"restless, shrewd eyes" of a grown woman, she is an anima figure who
incites in him polar feelings of love and hate. After making love with
her, he realizes she is "as human as any girl he had known" (chap. 17).
Then he wants to kill her because he realizes she has made him psychologically incapable of doing his job, killing androids. Nevertheless,
he *must* go on as a bounty hunter, thereby violating his identity, quash-
ing his empathy, and becoming more androidlike himself.

At one point Deckard is captured by android cops, who have formed
an alternate police department, claiming to be human and accusing
him of being an android. They introduce him to their own bounty
hunter, Phil Resch, who they claim is an android, but who thinks he
is human. When Resch later tests out as human, Deckard realizes he
would have killed him without compunction if Resch had turned out
to be android. Dick returns to the epistemological question he first
raised in "Impostor": how can we prove to ourselves we are real human
beings and not androids with implanted artificial memories? But further than that, he has Deckard realize that Resch is his shadowy double: a man who enjoys killing for its own sake, someone whose
humanity is compromised, despite his human status.

Although he does not kill Rachael, Deckard dispatches her exact
double, a cold, unsympathetic character named Pris, who recalls Pris
Frauenzimmer from *We Can Build You*. In fact, in his 1976 essay "Man,
Android and Machine" Dick makes the Pris-Rachael connection himself. Defining androids as "fierce cold things" which "have been some-

how generated to deceive us in a cruel way, to cause us to think it to be one of ourselves," he says:

> Like Rachael Rosen, they can be pretty but somehow lack something; or, like Pris in *We Can Build You,* they can be absolutely born of a human womb and even design androids—the Abraham Lincoln one in that book—and themselves be without warmth; they then fall within the clinical entity "schizoid," which means lacking proper feeling. . . . A human being without the proper empathy or feeling is the same as an android built so as to lack it, either by design or mistake. We mean, basically, someone who does not care about the fate which his fellow living creatures fall victim to; he stands detached, a spectator, acting out by his indifference John Donne's theorem that "No man is an island," but giving that theorem a twist: that which is a mental and moral island *is not a man.*[8]

In our world, Dick continues, the living is becoming more reified, while machines are becoming more like animate life. Our effort must be to grow beyond the mechanical, unconscious programming within us: "Each of us, then, partakes of the cosmos—if he is willing to listen to his dreams. And it is his dreams which will transform him from a mere machine into an authentic human.[9]

Deckard may be changed by his experience. He no longer wants to be a policeman; he feels like "nothing but a crude cop with crude cop hands" (chap. 22). Mercerism holds no attraction for him anymore: "fusion" seems to be an escape from and dulling of individual joy and pain, a homogenization of specific feeling. The ending of the novel is pure irony. Deckard seems to find redemption in the desert, near a hill like the one Mercer climbed. He finds a toad, a species which had been thought to be extinct. When he gets it back home, his wife discovers it is only electric. While he stumbles off disillusioned to bed, she orders some artificial flies for it, telling the clerk that her husband is devoted to the toad.

And why not? Perhaps the moral of *Do Androids Dream* is that the inanimate must be integrated with living consciousness. Love even androids, even electric toads. They stand for something as yet unassimilated in human nature. Must it be, as Mercer says, that "There is no salvation" (chap. 15), that man is born under the "curse" of having to do wrong and violate his own identity time and again? Dick never offers a vision of salvation, of eternal deliverance from the contradictions of existence, but he does offer hope for liberation from the cloud of ignorance that keeps people in misery. He affirms that we can stop being androids; that we can, by listening to our dreams, become fully human.

## Ubik

*Ubik* (written in 1966, published in 1969) is a landmark in Dick's development. Not only is it generally considered to be one of his best novels, it marks the first distinct appearance of the transcendental element in his work. Up until *Ubik,* he had been content to demonstrate that there is no "objective" reality irrespective of consciousness: the mind essentially constructs its own world. The shared world we live in is really a compromise, a blend of conflicting subjectivities, which under extraordinary circumstances reveal themselves as fundamentally different. To this anarchic viewpoint is added the concept of ultimate reality, beyond both subjectivity and objectivity. It is unified, uncreated, and absolute. It is what religion calls God, science calls the unified field, and Dick calls Ubik.

*Ubik* is told primarily from the point of view of Joe Chip, who works for an anti-psi organization headed by Glen Runciter. Its purpose is to use individuals with counter-talents to neutralize those with psi powers. Runciter communicates with his dead wife Ella, who is in "cold-pac," a kind of quick-freeze, suspended animation that greatly prolongs the remaining impulses of cephalic activity in those who have just died. Caught in a bomb blast, Joe recovers to find that the objects in his environment are regressing to a past state: a modern stereo becomes an old Victrola, current money reverts to obsolete issue, and so on. Joe even finds some of his coins carry the picture of Runciter, who supposedly died in the blast. He starts getting strange messages from Runciter in such forms as graffiti and television commercials. Gradually Joe realizes that it is he who is dead, not Runciter, and that his deteriorating world is a projection of his own mind as he lies in cold-pac. It is in effect a hallucination, one that is slipping away entropically with the precipitous aging of everything around him.

The inexorable entropic drift is a natural projection of dying awareness. Elsewhere Dick suggested that this regression to prior versions of objects represents a peeling back to a greater level of *reality,* to earlier manifestations of the underlying ideal Platonic forms.[10] One is reminded of the backward flow of time in *Counter-Clock World,* where the reversion indicates a purgatorial, pre-apocalyptic phase. In *Ubik* as well, death is a prelude to rebirth: the process of reincarnation described in *The Tibetan Book of the Dead* is a fact here.

Joe and other Runciter employees, also in cold-pac, are threatened with extinction by "An infantile, retarded entity . . . a polymorphic, perverse agency" (chap. 13) named Jory. Although merely a teenager in cold-pac who is "feeding" on the energy of other half-lifers, Jory becomes a kind of embodiment of evil like Palmer Eldritch, a force that in Dick's Gnostic view attempts to keep mankind deluded, suspended in a false reality. Jory does not represent death per se, which is only a phase in the evolutionary cycle; rather he is that which opposes evolution. He wants to freeze and extinguish life.

The only thing standing between Joe and this fate is a product called Ubik, which comes in spray cans, and, when sprayed on, instantly counteracts the forces of destruction. At the beginning of each chapter there is an advertisement for Ubik. For example: "Instant Ubik has all the fresh flavor of just-brewed drip coffee. Your husband will say, Christ, Sally, I used to think your coffee was only so-so. But now, wow! Safe when taken as directed" (chap. 3). Among other things, Ubik appears as a razor blade, a deodorant, a bra, a breakfast cereal, a pill for stomach relief, plastic wrap, a salad dressing, a used car, and a savings and loan. As its name implies, it is ubiquitous. Like the unified field, it pervades all relative manifestation, even the most ordinary objects. The recurrent theme in Dick of "the divine invasion," of the incursion of the unified field into the profane world of ignorance and entropy, is here quite clearly. The absolute pervades the relative; the sacred inhabits the profane. In the last chapter the true identity of Ubik is revealed:

I am Ubik. Before the universe was, I am. I made the suns. I made the worlds. I created the lives and the places they inhabit; I move them here, I put them there . . . I am the word and my name is never spoken, the name which no one knows. I am called Ubik, but that is not my name. I am. I shall always be. (chap. 17)

Dick's conception of the unified field is simultaneously scientific and religious. He sees Ubik as a source of negative entropy, of a higher degree of order upholding life. Entropy may be inexorable—the second law of thermodynamics will see to that—but Ubik's ubiquitous presence restores the vision of the unchanging law underlying the transitory and decaying.

Ubik as the spray can is the product of intelligence in the battle against evil. Though a symbol of the divine, it is not a mere magical aid; it has been invented by humans and can only be transferred through human hands, like a gift. Furthermore, it must be summoned up by the person who needs it by an exercise of will and intelligence. Joe Chip has to actively fight Jory, and in doing so he calls forth a beautiful young girl from the future who gives him a can of Ubik, which saves him from utter dissolution.

The ending of *Ubik* has a twist that seems to call into question the substantiality of the "real world" that is the reference point from which we are evaluating the events of half-life. Runciter, communicating to Joe Chip from the world of the living, finds that his own coins are beginning to carry Joe's image on them, in the same way that Joe's coins have converted to Runciter money. And as the final words of the novel indicate, "This was just the beginning" (chap. 17).

Critics have responded variously to this ending. Michael Bishop thinks it shows that Joe Chip's reality is primary; that Joe Chip is Everyman and subsumes the reality of Runciter and even the reader in his own.[11] Ian Watson says that Runciter may have been dead all along, "inside" rather than outside the half-life world.[12] Hazel Pierce thinks the Joe Chip coin is a sign that Runciter's own regression has begun; therefore, there is no help from "outside" for Chip because everything he has experienced is in his own head.[13]

Others have seen this ending as an invitation to step outside the universe of the novel and view it as a metafiction. Kim Stanley Robinson says that the final twist contradicts the "facts" of the rest of the narrative, making everything that came before impossible: "*Ubik* is, formally, the clearest example of Dick's plan of imbedding inconsistency in the structure of the text. Every reader of *Ubik* becomes engaged, just like its characters, in the struggle to create a coherent explanation of the events of the narrative, and like the characters every reader is eventually defeated."[14] Peter Fitting thinks the ending shows that "this kind of text is no longer a window opening into transcendental meaning, but a mirror which reflects the reader's perspective, forcing him out of his familiar reading habits while drawing his attention to the role of the novel as a form of manipulation" (i.e., coercing the reader to reduce the text to a "meaning").[15]

All of these interpretations are valid, but Dick's own, from "Man, Android and Machine," is perhaps the best:

. . . we are like the characters in my novel *Ubik*; we are in a state of half-life. We are neither dead nor alive, but preserved in cold storage, waiting to be thawed out. . . . ice and snow cover our world in layers of accretions, which we call *dokos* or Maya. What melts away the rind or layer of frozen ice over the world each year is of course the reappearance of sun. What melts the ice and snow covering the characters in *Ubik,* and which halts the cooling-off of their lives, the entropy which they feel, is the voice of Mr. Runciter, their former employer, calling to them. The voice of Mr. Runciter is none other than that same voice which each bulb and seed and root in the ground, our ground, in our wintertime, hears. It hears: "Wake up! Sleepers awake!"[16]

Elsewhere Dick has identified Ubik as Atman (the Supreme Self in Vedic philosophy) and Runciter is identified as the Logos (the active element of the divine; the Christ or redeemer).[17] But he is a human being, not a god. In his screenplay version of *Ubik,* written in 1974 but never filmed, Dick states that Runciter is "never fake"; he has an "abiding quality of the genuine" and "common sense."[18] Runciter, while he may be himself in half-life (whether in cold-pac, or meta-phorically, like all the rest of us), becomes in Dick's own view a human embodiment of the spirit of Ubik. Runciter's is an integrative con-sciousness that extends itself in empathy to others, to help them break through the veil of illusion. Yet he faces the necessity of going through the half-life state himself into full being.

We might say that at the end of *Ubik* the "real world" no longer has a privileged status: it is part of a larger field that includes the reality called half-life. Within this great network of interpenetrating con-sciousness, there is no hard and fast separation between minds and the objective realities they cooperatively structure. By the end of the novel Joe Chip's supposedly private reality, or *idios kosmos,* has begun to in-vade the *koinos kosmos,* as coins with his image on them mysteriously begin to appear in the common currency of the ordinary world of the living. This shows that the power of Ubik transcends the supposedly irreconcilable distinction between subjective and objective worlds. This causes the whole structure of the novel to become paradoxical, as is also true of a couple of other of Dick's best novels, *VALIS* and *The Man in the High Castle,* which are not reducible in terms of conven-tional analysis of narrative structure. They seem to constitute some kind of topological form as in an Escher drawing, with its own internal logic, completely self-referential, the equivalent of the paradoxical logic loop: "The following statement is true. The preceding statement is false." Such a construct is what Douglas Hofstadter, in *Godel, Escher, Bach,* calls a "Strange Loop."

The paradoxical structure of a Dick novel opens the awareness to the underlying order of the unified field, or *holomovement,* a word coined by physicist David Bohm. This holistic, flowing movement is "implicate" everywhere in the "explicate," four-dimensional space-time world of our senses. The holomovement enfolds matter and consciousness in a dynamic field of infinite correlation and self-referentiality: "the primary emphasis is now on *undivided wholeness,* in which the observing instrument is not separated from what is observed.[19]

Beyond consensual reality, beyond the private cosmos, and beyond even the archetypal *koinos kosmos,* lies the unified field. In modern physics the unified field represents the Grail wherein the conflict of opposites, the duality of force and matter fields, is finding its ultimate synthesis in the multidimensional theories of superspace, where general relativity and quantum theory attain their common ground. The spins of all particles previously thought distinct are now seen as having a hidden symmetry. What this means is that every possible manifestation of matter or energy is a breaking of that original symmetry, and everything can be understood in terms of its context in the unified field: in the words of physicist Paul Davies, "The world, it seems, can be built more or less out of structured nothingness."[20]

Dick's aim in *Ubik* is to reveal that structure as maya and thrust the ontological questions outside the structure of the novel and into the reader's reality—forcing him to ask, "Am I dead? Am I dreaming?" Clearly Dick believes that in a sense we all are.

## Galactic Pot-Healer

In *Galactic Pot-Healer* (1969) Dick's attention was more on creating a myth than on writing a novel. The characters are relatively undeveloped, and the science-fictional conceits are used rather casually as vehicles for archetypes; the work is almost a Jungian allegory. It does not lack Dick's characteristic humanizing touches, but its tendency toward myth makes it unique among his novels. It is certainly as dense with themes and ideas as any fiction he ever wrote.

Joe Fernwright, the hero, is found at the beginning in an oppressive future dystopia where policemen stop people for walking too slowly, all phone calls are monitored, and everyone is programmed to have a common dream every night. It is the ultimate Communist denial of personal consciousness: "the planetwide Party apparatus, the network of tendrils . . . had penetrated and then in loving convulsion clasped them in a hug of death as great as the entire world" (chap. 1). To escape this dreary reality, people lease encephalic gadgets that compel them to believe in the reality of the 3-D scene of California projected on their subsurface Cleveland windows. But Joe is a misfit; his mind is cut off from this consensual reality of pure illusion. Thus he is receptive to the strange messages he begins receiving from the Glimmung, a godlike, extraterrestrial being.

Joe's profession is pot-healing: he has the skill of not just mending but restoring broken pots to their exact original condition. The Glimmung enlists him on a team made up of species from throughout the galaxy to help raise a sunken cathedral called Heldscalla on the Glimmung's home world, Plowman's Planet. The Glimmung is a huge, amorphous, many-tendriled organism, whose power seems nearly unlimited and would seem to be merely a replacement for the Party (as described above) in Joe's life, another power to manipulate him—but the Glimmung's objective is different. Its aim is self-knowledge, both for itself and the creatures it has recruited. It explains that all life is one—"There are no small lives" (chap. 5)—and that Being is eternal. By doing something meaningful, one contacts that Being—one *is*.

The Glimmung can manifest in any form, and its appearance to Joe is an epiphany that changes his life:

. . . in Glimmung he witnessed eternal, self-renewing strength. Glimmung, like a star, fed on himself, and was never consumed. And, like a star, he was beautiful; he was a fountain, a meadow, an empty twilight street over which dwelt a fading sky. The sky would fade; the twilight would become darkness, but Glimmung would blaze on, as if burning out the impurities of everyone and everything around him. He was the light who exposed the soul and all its decayed parts. And, with that light, he scorched out of existence those decayed portions, here and there: mementos of a life not asked for (chap. 5).

The Glimmung, in its eternality, is an image of the Absolute, as was Ubik. The Glimmung can communicate directly on the level of consciousness with many beings simultaneously, creating alternate realities in their minds. But it is a god, it is one that is broken and must be healed; and it needs lesser finite beings to help it effect its own evolution. It is certainly not particularly a god of love; it acts more like a wrathful, egotistical, Old Testament deity. This is because it is fragmented from its original unity: there is a Black Glimmung, its deadly antagonist, and a sunken Black Cathedral as well. The Glimmung's freedom seems to be circumscribed by the Fatelike Kalends, whose Book (like Dr. Bloode's text in *The Unteleported Man*) forecasts everything that will happen on Plowman's Planet. So in many ways the Glimmung's need to integrate the dark side of its nature and transcend the determinism of relative existence parallels Joe's quest to apply his pot-healing skill on his "fallen," fragmented self.

The Glimmung is seen as Faustian because, like Faust, it is trying to reclaim from the sea a "new earth"—which in this case is the raising of Heldscalla. Symbolically, the raising of the sunken cathedral is the resurrection of the buried, divine aspect of self—both Joe's and the Glimmung's. This is an initiatory journey for both man and god, involving a symbolical death and rebirth. Joe, diving to survey Heldscalla, enters a realm beyond time and discourses with his own corpse, which tells him he must help raise the cathedral in order to release it from its state of limbo, of half-life. In Jungian terms, this encounter with the Shadow, or unconscious dark side of the self, parallels the Glimmung's battle with the Black Glimmung. The Faustian quest to raise the unconscious to consciousness results in a showdown that the Glimmung wins. But this winning simply means that the shadow of ignorance has passed, and that the unconscious part of the self has been assimilated in a higher integration.

The encounter with the anima is also a part of the individuation process. Joe's anima, represented by the beautiful Mali Jojez, strikes him as a contrast to his wife, a castrating bitch; but Mali's hostility toward him throughout the novel indicates that Joe will always force a woman to play the bitch. It is only by withdrawing his anima projection from her that he can escape that syndrome. For the Glimmung, the anima encounter means realizing its bisexual nature. It changes from male to female and gives birth to a child-creature, which is the cathedral. This is the culmination of the healing of its fragmented self, the restoration of its unfallen androgynous divinity.

At the end of the novel nearly all the members of the Undertaking are absorbed by the Glimmung into a group mind; Joe leaves Mali behind and chooses individuality, or in Jungian terms, individuation. He takes a new step forward in re-creating himself: instead of being a healer of pots, he will be a pot maker. Even though the first pot he makes is "awful," it represents a breakthrough. For it is better to strive, Faustlike, and fail, than not to try. With the act of creation comes self-knowledge. Joe is not a god like the Glimmung, but he has awakened. He is on his way to becoming an enlightened human being.

## A Maze of Death

Completed in 1968 and published in 1970, *A Maze of Death* is a strange mixture of science fiction, mystery, and theology. Fourteen people are assigned to colonize an uninhabited planet, Delmak-O. One by one, they meet mysterious deaths. It is unclear whether the malevolent agent is a military conspiracy, evil aliens, or each other. The solution of this puzzle is, however, in the end less important than the mystery of Delmak-O itself.

Delmak-O gives indications of being a false reality; some of its life forms are organic, others are mechanical contraptions of unknown origin. Its central mystery is a monolithic Building that each member of the group sees in a different light. The lettering above the entrance changes according to the psychology of the viewer. The Building is the ultimate symbol, an irreducible core reality, that cannot be entered and whose nature can only be inferred. It underscores the colonists' alienation from each other: they are all in some sense failures, withdrawn into their private worlds. All have obsessions that keep them in their own *idios kosmos*. The leader of the group, Glen Belsnor, suspects they are all insane and are really subjects of a psychological experiment. This theory is borne out by Seth Morley, who explores Delmak-O, only to find that it not an alien world at all but an abandoned Earth.

The characters in this novel inhabit a universe where religion really works. The universally accepted theology is based on an apparently crackpot book—*How I Rose from the Dead in My Spare Time and So Can You* by A. J. Specktowsky, the great twenty-first-century Communist theologian. It describes God as having three aspects: The Mentufacturer, who creates and perpetually renews all things; the Intercessor, a Christlike revealer of ultimate reality; and the Walker-on-Earth, who often manifests as a human being to give aid to individuals. Opposed to the deity is the Form Destroyer, who represents entropy and decay. Prayers to God really work—as in the religious fanatic's dream cosmos in *Eye in the Sky*. In this case they must be transmitted electronically through a network of "god-worlds."

Specktowsky is vague as to whether the Form Destroyer is an antagonist on an equal footing with the three-personed deity, or rather its fourth aspect. The group's mystic, Tony Dunkelwelt, claims to commune with a god-above-god, beyond any of these manifestations. In his view, this higher god contains all categories including its opposite. This corresponds to the radical transcendentalism of gnosticism, where the spirit of dualism present in orthodox Christianity (and which bothered Jung) is resolved in the notion of a god beyond good and evil, utterly unmanifest. Dunkelwelt, however, is hardly more enlightened than anyone else in the group, for he kills an old man who he thinks is the Form Destroyer, who wins by means of illusion, making what is not real seem real.

When another character, Maggie Walsh, meets her death, she experiences a vision of afterlife that corresponds with the description in *The Tibetan Book of the Dead* where one passes through a frozen hell-world. That state recurs in many other Dick novels, including *The Man in the High Castle, Do Androids Dream of Electric Sheep?*, and *Ubik*. Maggie's search for an appropriate womb to be reborn in culminates in her absorption in a clear white light. In the author's foreword Dick states that this journey corresponded "in exact detail" with one of his own LSD trips.

In the final chapters the truth about Delmak-O comes out. After all of the members of the group have died, it is revealed that they dreamed the world of Delmak-O and are still alive inside a starship, which due to an accident is taking them on a lifelong trip. The fourteen group members had programmed a computer to create an illusory reality for them while they lay linked up in common, forming a "polyencephalic mind." This particular program involved their working out their accumulated hostilities, but to an extreme—it led to their killing each other. It constituted a diversion so they could keep their sanity in their spaceship prison. The space travelers are addicted to living in these dreamworlds—like the Mars colonists with the Perky Pat game in *The Three Stigmata of Palmer Eldritch*—so they quickly plug themselves back into the computer.

The Specktowsky theology was as unreal as Delmak-O, part of the computer's creation, and therefore the religious experiences of the group were also part of the illusion. The real Specktowsky was their ship's captain who had died, playing something of the role Runciter played for the half-lifers in *Ubik*, impinging on their imaginary reality like a god to give them spiritual succor. But just as *Ubik* ended with a twist that called into question the supposed "primary reality," so *A Maze of Death* ends with an appearance of the Intercessor in the primary reality of the spaceship. The deity extends itself outside the polyencephalic mind to prevent Seth Morley from taking the lives of himself and the others while they lie in mental fusion, transported to a new version of Delmak-O. The Intercessor soothes Morley's troubled mind by granting him one thousand years of life as a plant. Delmak-O is a metaphor for consensual reality, the lowest common denominator of reality that a group can agree on, but that does not provide a true meeting ground for the private, obsessive universes of individuals, their personal *idios kosmos*. Morley's experience shows that it is possible to break through the personal and social limitations on consciousness to the *koinos kosmos,* or archetypal reality, the realm of the gods.

Kim Stanley Robinson sees *A Maze of Death* as "one of the blackest and most bitter moments in Dick's career."[21] He thinks that the appearance of the Intercessor at the end, outside of the common hallucination, only supports the air of desperation because the sole escape from the "endless horror" of the starship the characters are trapped on is a miracle. Such is the critic's distrust of miracles that when they happen, as in this case, they prove that things are even worse than we thought them to be! Dick is not as relentlessly ironic as his critics. By the Intercessor's appearance a supposed fiction comes to life. Divinity exists, and manifests in a timely way to give Seth Morley the blessed rest that he needs. Whatever else this may be, it is not desperation.

## Our Friends from Frolix 8

Dick's next novel was in a sense a throwback. *Our Friends from Frolix 8* was completed in 1969 and published in paperback the following year by Ace Books during a period when Dick was getting initial hardcover publication for most of his other novels. Its heavy emphasis on the personalities of power politicians recalls *The Simulacra, Now Wait for Last Year,* and *The Penultimate Truth.* Its theme of an Earthman returning from a long space voyage with an alien possessed of superpowers recalls *The Three Stigmata of Palmer Eldritch,* and the character of the heartless young girl who seduces the protagonist is Pris from *We Can Build You* recycled. Dick himself called the novel a "throwaway," a "regression," "simply written for money."[22]

The plot is a little thin compared to the density and dazzling complexity of the books of the early 1960s, and perhaps a bit of weariness at the standard conventions of science fiction is showing. The style is slack and the characters have a tendency to babble:

"You're a good man, Council Chairman," Barnes said. "To extend your loyalties even to those who are now actively working against you."

"I'm a slimy bastard," Gram grated. "You know it; I know it. It's just that—well, hell. We had a lot of good times together; we used to get a million laughs out of what we printed. Laughs, because we put funny stuff into it. Now it's all solemn and stodgy. But when I was there, we—aw, the hell with it." He lapsed into silence. *What am I doing here?* he asked himself. *How did I get into a position like this, with all this authority? I never was meant for it.*

On the other hand, he thought, *maybe I was.* (chap. 11)

As Paul Williams says, "Phil's characters say whatever comes into their heads."[23] Yet Dick's apparent casualness about controlling the plot and characters is more endearing than irritating. We may not prize *Our Friends from Frolix 8* as a masterpiece of structure, but it is typical Dick, involving and entertaining.

The story is set in a world controlled by superintelligent "New Men" and telepathic "Unusuals," who reign despotically together over the "Old Men," or ordinary, unevolved humans. Gram is the ruthless world leader, possessed by self-doubts and therefore somewhat sympathetic, though he is plotting to kill his wife. Also having problems with his wife, but on the other end of the social spectrum, is Nick Appleton, a mere tire regroover, who has unknowingly been singled out as the statistically significant average man. When he joins the Undermen, the political underground, and falls in love with Charlotte, sixteen-year-old "gutter rat" revolutionary, he comes to Gram's attention. Is a mass defection of Old Men to the rebellion at hand?

In the course of the novel Thors Provini returns to earth with a "friend" for the Old Men in the form of a telepathic, protoplasmic alien with extraordinary powers. A benevolent sort of Palmer Eldritch, this godlike being overthrows the government by depriving the Unusuals of their special powers with one stroke, and by regressing the New Men to a childlike state of mind. Amos Ild, the world's highest intellect, designer of the Great Ear, an electronic mind-reading device that would have been the ultimate totalitarian tool, is reduced to drawing stick figures on pieces of paper.

Another New Man, formerly a lawyer, voices an uncharacteristic sense of wonder: "Can God fly? Can He hold out His arms and fly? . . . Someday . . . I think every living thing will fly or anyhow trudge or run . . . Up and up. Forever. Even slugs and snails; they'll go very slow but they'll make it sometime. All of them will make it eventually, no matter how slow they go. Leaving a lot behind; that has to be done" (chap. 27). This is a vision of the evolution of consciousness of every living thing on the planet toward some unimaginable fulfillment. The Frolixan has assisted, but Dick is not saying we are ultimately dependent upon such semidivine intervention. The whole process is cosmic and inexorable; and it depends as surely on the exercise of individual free will and intelligence as on extraterrestrial grace. It depends on the courage of people like Nick, who gives up his safe, predictable routine for the complete uncertainty of life with Charlotte and the Undermen.

The amorphous Frolixan, like the protoplasmic Lord Running Clam in *Clans of the Alphane Moon,* represents the egoless moral integrity toward which humanity is rising. Nick may be a long way from that level of perfection and power, but someday, Dick implies, the little guy will get here, and then God will be flesh.

## *Flow My Tears, the Policeman Said*

*Flow My Tears, the Policeman Said* was published in 1974, but it can be considered as belonging with the novels of the late 1960s. According to Paul Williams, a complete draft was finished by August, 1970.[24] Dick stated in an interview that the book was "essentially written" by that time: he typed up the final version in 1973 adding only "stylistic touches."[25] In terms of subject matter, the novel has much in common with works such as *Eye in the Sky* and *Ubik,* where the twisted mind-set of a character alters the objective reality of others in his environment. *Flow My Tears* is a masterfully executed, powerful treatment of this theme.

The premise of this novel is that by taking a toxic drug called KR-3 one can become "unbound in space" and start to inhabit alternate spatial corridors branching off from the "real" one. A latent possibility is substituted for the actual, and objects of one's percept system are altered as well as one's subjective awareness. When Alys Buckman, a malevolent, sadomasochistic power-tripper, thoroughly decadent in all matters of sex and drugs, takes KR-3, she is able to pull Jason Taverner, popular TV entertainer, into an alternate reality where no one except her knows who he is. Jason is an unknowing object of fantasy for Alys. When he is sucked into her "irreal" KR-3 world, he is confronted with the ultimate humiliation for someone whose sense of self is defined by public acclaim—to be a nobody.

Jason must survive as a nonperson in a police state where to be caught without identification can mean spending the rest of one's life in a forced-labor camp. The focus is on his relationship with several women: Heather Hart, his famous girlfriend, who no longer knows him when he loses his identity; Marilyn Mason, a jilted lover who tries to kill him; Kathy, a psychotic police informer; Ruth Rae, an unhappy, sex-starved barfly; and Mary Ann Dominic, an innocent child of the sixties who continues to live in a world of Buffy St. Marie and pottery-making. All of them come under his spell, for unlike most Dick protagonists, Jason has personal charisma, sexual magnetism, and self-confidence. A genetically engineered superior type called a "six," he manages rather well against the crushing odds of an omnipotent police-state apparatus, and he earns the reader's respect. But he is also an egotist, a man who uses women and who has advanced his TV career ruthlessly. In a sense he is destined for his fall from grace, into ignominy. Each woman he meets inflicts a wound, teaching him something about the vacuousness of his loveless soul.

Love is portrayed throughout the novel as a form of attachment. It is symbolized by the gelatinous Callisto cuddle sponge, with its deadly feeding tubes, that Marilyn Mason plants on Jason's chest. Kathy, who makes false identification papers for Jason, attempts to entrap him in her own fashion; her love is like a "tender vine" and the identity he gains through such an unstable source is short-lived. Ruth vainly uses the tried and true avenue of sex to entice lasting love. Alys's love, which through KR-3 pulls Jason into her universe, is the strongest manipulative power in the novel. But all of these unreal manifestations of love fail. What endures is the spirit of the loving heart, which Mary Anne possesses in her simplicity and which is represented in her art.

If a change in one person's consciousness can alter reality for everyone else, it means that reality is a consciousness-produced phenomenon and that individual minds are interlinked in its production. Jason's "star" status is the reference point for his reality. When he wakes up in a world that doesn't know who he is, people think he's insane, suffering from delusions of grandeur. Kathy, a schizoid, thinks maybe she has invented him, a celebrity that no one has heard of, and he accuses her of solipsism. But Jason's dependency on his celebrity status makes him a solipsist too, because the universe has shifted and he hasn't. In his mind, it still revolves around him. He is wrong, but Alys is a solipsist who happens to be right, for she makes Jason a performer on the stage of her mind, and her mind only.

Later, Jason conjectures that his whole career as a TV star had been a drug-induced hallucination. The truth is the opposite; the world in which he is not a star is a hallucination. But the two realities seem to cancel each other out. They are founded on the same shifting sands—an identity that lacks depth and internal coherence. By contrast, Mary Anne Dominic is a grounded person. A maker of beautiful pots (always a virtue in Dick), she has no desire for fame, but is content in her work—which in an Epilogue turns out to be the only thing that endures, for all the characters are seen to meet their ends eventually. Mary Anne doesn't want to be like Jason, who is always questioning his identity. She is secure in aspiring to quality on a small scale. She knows she's real, a self-knowledge Jason lacks because his identity rests on the consensus of other people. If they agree with him that he's a celebrity, he's sane; if they don't, he's insane. It's a precarious method of living one's life. Small wonder he is so susceptible to being drawn into Alys's *idios kosmos*.

In the latter part of the novel the focus shifts to police general Felix Buckman, Alys's brother, who coincidentally has become interested, and baffled, by the Taverner case. He lives incestuously with his sister, whose self-destructive, degenerate life-style represents the exact opposite of the rational, controlling position he holds. Because his job is essentially dehumanizing, he is alienated from his feeling side, and Alys compensates for that imbalance as a vengeful anima. She systematically tries to undermine him, and her manipulation of Jason into his nonperson status, beyond police control, is a slap in Felix's face. She shows that she can alter elements in his world that reduce his reality structure to a meaningless joke.

In the end, after Alys's death from KR-3, Felix has been purged of her evil influence and begins to regain touch with his feeling side. In a lonely gas station he encounters a stranger, a black man, to whom he hands a piece of paper with a picture of a heart pierced by an arrow. Then he hugs the man. It is a significant step toward embracing his "shadow" side, the unrealized potential, that the black man tends to symbolize in the white psyche. Felix, whose name means "happy" in Latin, may be beginning to discover, in an uncharacteristic flow of tears, the love that will redeem him. Indeed, toward the end of his life, we are told, he writes a book exposing and criticizing the planetwide police system.

The words "Flow My Tears" come from a John Dowland song that is cited in the novel as the first piece of abstract music. Aside from the fact that Dick loved Elizabethan songs, this connection is significant because pure abstract beauty such as Dowland's song and Mary Anne's pots point toward an ideal form that partakes of the unified field beyond the *idios kosmos* of the individual. There is something absolute and Platonic about them. Their presence in our world is like the spray can of Ubik that rescues all of us from the daily hallucination we call life.

## Short Fiction of the 1960s

Although Dick's productivity in the shorter forms declined considerably in the 1960s as he concentrated on novels, he did publish over twenty short stories and novelettes during these years. Some were expanded into novels: "Cantata 140" became *The Crack in Space*; "Novelty Act" became *The Simulacra*; "Your Appointment Will Be Yesterday" became *Counter-Clock World*. Other stories contributed important elements to the novels: the Perky Pat game in "The Days of Perky Pat" to *The Three Stigmata of Palmer Eldritch*; the empathy religion of Mercerism in "The Little Black Box" to *Do Androids Dream of Electric Sheep?*; the half-lifers in "What the Dead Men Say" to *Ubik*.

Several of the stories of this period concern memory as a reality-structuring device. In "We Can Remember It for You Wholesale" a man who tries to have false memories implanted in him that will make him believe he has been to Mars as a secret agent learns that he really did go to Mars in that capacity, and his real memories were erased by the authorities. Subjectively, the difference between the true and false memories amounts to nothing: they are equally real. "Retreat Syndrome" features a man who suffers from a self-induced delusion that he killed his wife. When confronted with her alive, he tries again and again to kill her, to make reality conform to his false memory. In "Precious Artifact" a man is psychologically influenced to believe that an Earth devastated by war is still populated; his need to cling to the prewar memory contributes to constructing a believable hallucination.

Perhaps the best of Dick's stories, "The Electric Ant" is a profound exploration of the idea that consciousness structures reality. A man who discovers himself to be an organic robot tinkers with the mechanism that projects, like a motion picture, his external world. Finally he determines to cut the punched tape running in his chest in order to discover the "ultimate and absolute reality," with this result:

He saw apples and cobblestones and zebras. He felt warmth, the silky texture of cloth; he felt the ocean lapping at him and a great wind, from the north, plucking at him as if to lead him somewhere. . . . Butter relaxed into liquid on his tongue, and at the same time hideous odors and tastes assailed him: the bitter presence of poisons and lemons and blades of summer grass. He drowned; he fell; he lay in the arms of a woman in a vast white bed which at the same time dinned shrilly in his ear: the warning noise of a defective elevator in one of the ancient, ruined downtown hotels. I am living, I have lived, I will never live, he said to himself. . . .

The perceptions that flood in when he cuts off his programming "kill" him, if a robot can be said to die. He ceases to experience, and when he does, his secretary sees her world begin to dissolve as well. The disappearance of objective reality, here as at the end of *Ubik,* under-scores Dick's conviction that objects of perception are dependent on consciousness—even a machine's consciousness—for their very exis-tence. There is no absolute reality in anybody's relative perceptions.

The theme of reality breakdown is also central of "Faith of Our Fa-thers," which originally appeared in Harlan Ellison's tradition-break-ing anthology *Dangerous Visions* (1967). In a future world communist state a young bureaucrat named Chien, under the influence of an an-tihallucinogen, discovers that the Absolute Benefactor of the People is an utterly evil alien entity. Others hallucinate it as human because they are perpetually drugged through the water supply. This Palmer Eld-ritch-like being is the personification of death, and has godlike power. If we refer to the Gnostic philosophy that underlies this story and all of Dick's work, the Absolute Benefactor as "God" is really the demi-urge, creator of the relative world and the spell of ignorance under which all inevitably fall. The ending is uncharacteristically bleak for Dick: the young man is doomed to die because the Thing has touched him. Even here, though, he finds some last solace through making love to a woman; he experiences a glimpse of unity before being con-sumed by the unknown terror. But it is not easy to turn "Faith of Our Fathers" into a positive vision. Along with *A Scanner Darkly,* it is Dick's deepest descent into darkness.

# Chapter Six

# The Seventies and Eighties

## "The Dark-Haired Girl"

From 1970 through the end of Dick's life his writing veered away from science fiction, even the idiosyncratic vein he had been mining, and became simultaneously more autobiographical and metaphysical. He went for long periods without writing any fiction. In late 1972 he put together a manuscript consisting of a series of letters he had written from March through October of that year, entitling it "The Dark-Haired Girl: A Search for the Other." It had not yet been published at this writing, but there are plans to do so.

The letters cover Dick's relationships with four "dark-haired girls," the last of whom, Tessa, became his fifth wife and brought to a culmination his quest for the ideal woman—at least for a few years. Certainly it was more than coincidental that he got involved with so many dark-haired girls, for they had been populating his fiction since the beginning, as innocents or temptresses or both. Dick projected his own complex needs on the fictional and real women in this category: they represented a powerful aspect of his anima that probably was connected with his ability to create. In one letter about Tessa he wrote: "the girl gave substance to the reality outside his own head. She was an external point, a fixed spot of being that he had not merely imagined. Out of her permanence—much more actual than his own—a field of lesser sturdiness spread to every object and thing. . . ." The woman was an anchor to external reality and inspired him to manifest his vision in external terms—to write his novels. After meeting Tessa he left behind two difficult and unproductive years and began to write again.

"The Dark-Haired Girl" is interesting not only from the standpoint of biography, but for Dick's attempts to draw universal truths from his own experience. He built his philosophy from the ground up, based on his sensitivity to the relativity of different points of view. He was capable of seeing the world as a "multiple reality, as if half hallucination and [half] objective reality," which "can be said to be both true and untrue at any given moment." Thus he extrapolated the Uncertainty Principle as the key to living in the rapidly changing present:

> If two people dream the same dream it ceases to be an illusion: the sole prior test that distinguished reality from hallucination was the consensus gentium, that one other or several others saw it, too. This is the idios kosmos, the private dream, contrasted to the shared dream of us all, the koinos kosmos. What is new in our time is that we are beginning to see the plastic, trembling quality of the koinos kosmos—which scares us, its insubstantiality—and the more-than-mere-vapor quality of the hallucination. Like s.f., a third reality is formed half way between.[1]

In this age it is no longer good enough, then, to rely on the consensual point of view to know reality. One must wake up from the private dream into the archetypal shared dream—behind which dwells the Absolute, the unified field that Dick exhaustively tried to approach in his later writings.

## A Scanner Darkly

*A Scanner Darkly* is Dick's dark night of the soul, and it is based on one of the lowest points in his life—his involvement with drugs and hard-drug users in 1970–72. Shortly after dropping out of the drug culture in early 1972, he began to set down his experiences. The novel was finished in 1975 and finally published in 1977. Dick gave great credit to his editor at Del Rey Books, Judy-Lynn del Rey, for helping him to learn how to create truly believable characters during the rewriting process.[2] Although Dick's characters had rarely been two-dimensional, in this novel they clearly take on flesh, and for him it was a breakthrough. The dialogue is street talk of the late 1960s, gritty and realistic; although the setting is Southern California in 1994, the science-fictional elements are minimal. More than ever Dick's characters say whatever comes into their heads—and never has it been more appropriate to the subject matter of the book: the psychology of minds deteriorating through the use of drugs. The conversations reflect, often humorously, the derangement of the characters.

The novel is ferociously antidrug, but as Dick insists in the concluding Author's Note, this is not a "bourgeois" novel that preaches and moralizes against deviant behavior: "it does not say they were wrong to play when they should have toiled; it just tells what the consequences were." Dick adds a list of his friends, on whom the fictional characters are based, and the consequences they suffered: in all cases, physical breakdown, mental derangement, or death. He is on the list himself with "permanent pancreatic damage." It was Dick's primary intention to express his love for his friends; not to portray them as either victims or vermin, but simply to remember them: "These were comrades whom I had; there are no better. They remain in my mind, and the enemy will never be forgiven. The 'enemy' was their mistake in playing. Let them all play again, in some other way, and let them be happy."

Dick's compassion for his characters is one of the few relieving factors in a pessimistic book. The very structure of the narrative implies that there is no way out: a tight circle of death imprisons people and forces them back to feed on themselves. The protagonist, Bob Arctor, is an addict of the hallucinogenic Substance D, nicknamed "Death." At the same time he is a narcotics agent named Fred whose job it is to spy on the illicit activities of his friends and himself through a sophisticated system of holoscanners that have been planted in his house. As Substance D causes the link between the two hemispheres of Arctor's brain to deteriorate, he literally forgets that he is leading a double life. He forgets whether he is a narc posing as a doper or a doper posing as a narc. His paranoid tendencies become more pronounced, and he loses the ability to speak and think logically. The internal split in his identity finally brings him to a crisis: he enters a drug rehabilitation center named New-Path that breaks down what is left of his fractured ego. He becomes a hebephrenic, as simple as a little child, with a new name ("Bruce") and very little memory of the nightmare period of his addiction.

The title of the novel derives from St. Paul's disquisition on love: "For now we see through a glass, darkly; but then face to face: now I know in part, but then shall I know even as also I am known" (I Corinthians 13:12). In the novel, looking in the scanner is the way Arctor (as Fred) knows himself; as he watches the holotapes of himself, the split in his personality increases and he sees more and more "in part," or only partially. The observing ego, turned on itself, fragments. Arctor is unable to see himself except as an object. In so doing he loses coordination between the rational, linear consciousness of his left brain and the spatial, intuitive right brain. Left-brained Fred splits off altogether from right-brained Arctor. Then, both "die" because they cannot exist independently. The only thing left to do at that point is to start over, and Bruce is the reborn child. But he is a child that may never grow into an intelligent adult again. Within the bounds of the novel there is no saving grace because the use of drugs has ruined Arctor's life beyond redemption.

Donna Hawthorne, Arctor's girlfriend, is sympathetically portrayed for a Dick woman, although she feels herself subject to the android syndrome: "Warm eyes, warm face, warm fucking fake smile, but inside I am cold all the time, and full of lies" (chap. 14). For unknown to Arctor, she too is an undercover narcotics agent, who while addicting him to Substance D has maneuvered him into a position where he can spy for the government on New-Path's activities.

The main science-fictional element in the story is a "scramble suit" that turns one into a vague blur, effectively concealing the narcs' true identity from each other. It contributes to Arctor's instability, for he begins to feel he has no real identity. The narcs are dehumanized and alienated by the institution that employs them, for society itself is schizophrenic in *A Scanner Darkly*. The "straight" mentality is one of severe repression of the play urges that those it defines as deviants, the "freaks," act out. The form this play takes is destructive partly because those isolated from the mainstream are under unconscious pressure to compensate for the lack of feeling in society as a whole, and thus are driven to extremes.

Dick viewed drug rehabilitation centers as one of the many manifestations of the totalitarian state, which he felt was the "greatest menace of the twentieth century."[3] In this novel New-Path uses group attack therapy to break down the subject's ego—thus everything connected with their old life, including the drug habit. But the price paid is great. The personality is relentlessly reprogrammed to obey authority. And New-Path, which is apparently growing the flower from which Substance D is made, uses its victims to help perpetuate itself. This irony completes a circle that encloses all the characters in the novel, dopers and narcs alike. There is no exit; the finality is terrible. Never did Dick write with such fierce conviction, emotional power, and sense of grief as in this shattering novel.

## Deus Irae

*Deus Irae* began in 1964 as a forty-eight page manuscript by Dick entitled "The Kneeling Legless Man." Roger Zelazny, one of the most dazzling new science-fiction writers of the sixties, then entered as a collaborator. They passed new chapters back and forth, with the larger part being written by Zelazny; eventually the project was completed in 1975 and published the following year. Dick claimed he needed help from someone who knew about Christianity, since the story had a Christian theme,[4] but Zelazny did not significantly expand on the theological issues opened up in Dick's early fragment, which closely corresponds with the first three chapters and a bit of the fourth in the finished novel.

In a post-World-War-III wasteland a religion has grown up around the God of Wrath, whose human embodiment is supposedly Carleton Lufteufel, the government official who detonated the doomsday device that contaminated the Earth's atmosphere with radioactivity. Limbless painter Tibor McMaster sets off in his cart on a quest to find Lufteufel to capture the god's true visage in a painting. After various adventures, he finds Lufteufel and kills him, not knowing his true identity, and is fooled into thinking an old wino is the god instead. The resultant painting is henceforth taken as a definitive likeness of the god by the Servants of Wrath, who worship him while hating his evil power over all the world. To them, death represents the only freedom from bondage.

A vitiated Christianity encounters this life-negating religion rather feebly. The resolution of the two philosophies comes not through doctrine but, as one might expect in Dick, through vision. Pete Sands, a Christian, converses with the True God as a pot named Oh Ho (a pot actually owned by Dick). In the ending (which Dick said he wrote) Father Abernathy sees the world suddenly renewed, following the death of Lufteufel; the "occlusion" is lifted. Ignorance has departed, and glimpses of the "real," unspoiled world come seeping in. It would seem the Servants of Wrath cannot endure since their god has proved to be only a man. But this conclusion leaves an earlier scene, in which Tibor encountered the god in all his power, rather problematical.

Given the caliber of the coauthors, the novel is a disappointment; the whole is less than the sum of the parts. Dick grafted a couple of early stories, "The Great C" and "Planet for Transients," onto the account of Tibor's journey, making the story more episodic and less cohesive. The characters lack passion and the narrative has little drive. In comparison to *Dr. Bloodmoney*, the Dick novel that it most resembles, *Deus Irae* suffers. In both, there is a post-nuclear-war scenario, a limbless character in a mechanical cart, and an evil genius with unexplained powers who caused the war. But Tibor and Lufteufel are dead on the page, whereas Hoppy and Bloodmoney come alive and are remembered. Dick himself did not take the project very seriously, calling it "just an amateur thing that we were doing just for the pleasure of it."[5] That *Deus Irae* was finished at all under the circumstances is perhaps the greatest fact of note about it.

## The "Exegesis"

The great work that occupied Dick from 1974 until his death has not been published. He called it his "Exegesis"; it consists of two file cabinets filled with mostly handwritten pages, about two million words in all. Dick's purpose in it was to formulate theories to explain his experiences beginning in March 1974 that he interpreted as communications from a higher being called Valis or Zebra. This revelation became the central pivot upon which he viewed the meaning of his life and works:

> Without knowing it during the years I wrote, my thinking & writing was a long journey toward enlightenment. I first saw the illusory nature of space when I was in high school. In the late forties I saw that Causality was an illusion. Later, during my 27 years of published writing, I saw the mere hallucinatory nature of [the] world. & also of self (& memories). Year after year, book after book & story, I shed illusion after illusion: self, time, space, causality, world—I finally sought (in 1970) to know what *was* real. Four years later, at my darkest moment of dread & trembling, my ego crumbling away, I was granted Dibba Cakkhu—&, although I did not realize it at the time, I became a Buddha . . . All illusion dissolves away like a soap bubble & I saw reality at last—& in the 4 1/2 years since, have at last comprehended it intellectually—i.e. what I saw & knew & experienced (my exegesis).[6]

Much of the "Exegesis" is devoted to analysis of Dick's own novels as anticipating the Valis revelations, for Dick believed he had unconsciously written about the events of the 1970s in the 1960s.

The "Exegesis" is involved with metaphor-building around the basic conflict between cosmic good and evil that informs most of his work, from *The Cosmic Puppets* through *Palmer Eldritch* and *Ubik*. Ubik, Dick decided, was a power identical with Valis, a foreshadowing of the 1974 experience. While Valis was the "Macro Mind," Dick himself was "a micro-Pluriform of the Logos," impregnated with the "plasmate," or divine essence. By attacking him through various conspiracies, Satan would trap the divine Logos, which would then assimilate Satan's dominion, the world. Dick did not see himself as unique: every human being was Valis in seed form, but most were "occluded," or ignorant, of their true selves, and under the sway of the forces of "astral determinism."

Dick's sources for his philosophical speculations included gnosticism, kabbalah, Orphism, Neoplatonism, Buddhism, the Bible from the standpoint of esoteric Christianity, and *The Tibetan Book of the Dead*. He tried to synthesize all these influences and "derived a single sensationally revolutionary occult doctrine out of them."[7] Gnosticism was more appealing to him than orthodox Christianity because Dick rejected the doctrine of original sin. The Gnostic idea that mankind is simply ignorant of its essential nature, and that Satan *is* ignorance, provided the ideal theoretic basis for his thought-adventures. The Creator of the world is really the creator of a mass-hallucination of external reality, which causes people to forget their true selves. The myth of the Fall has nothing to do with sin; it simply outlines the process of fragmentation of consciousness into an occluded state, from which Valis redeems us: "Our real nature—forgotten but not lost—is that of being fallen or captured bits of the Godhead, whom the Savior restores to the Godhead. His nature—the Savior's—& ours is identical; we are him and he is us."[8]

Dick was never totally comfortable with the dualism encouraged in some Gnostic writings, which identified YHWH, the Old Testament God, as Satan. In a 1980 passage Dick says that Valis is not just the transcendental invader into the astrally determined order of the world—Valis is also God the creator: "What I saw that I called 'Valis' is probably Natura Naturens: the will of God, expressed directly on the field of physical reality (natura naturata).[9] Though he spun many competing theories throughout the "Exegesis," Dick eventually tried to resolve dualistic complications and view the action of Valis as part of the normal governance of God over the cosmos. The relative world, he felt, "serves a divine purpose: it teaches us, & we either learn or we do not. If we solve the moral & epistemological puzzles we get to return to the Godhead from which we came."[10] Valis is a fail-safe mechanism to get man out of the maze, the "Black Iron Prison" he has built for himself. The Savior is none other than ourselves, saving us from ourselves. That ultimate Faustian, heroic project leads to an apocalyptic goal: "the final triumph of the evolving spirit over matter, world and Fate, involving thousands of years of evolution towards 'Anokhi'— self awareness . . . pure consciousness."[11]

### *Radio Free Albemuth*

Although *Deus Irae* gave some glimpses of the issues that preoccupied Dick in the "Exegesis," the full impact of his transformed consciousness did not become apparent until the Valis novels. The first of these was entitled *Valisystem A* in manuscript, written in the summer of 1976, and finally published as *Radio Free Albemuth* in 1985. Although Mark Hurst, an editor at Bantam Books, accepted the novel for publication in 1976, retitling it *Valis*, Dick was discouraged by his minimal suggestions for revision and put the manuscript aside.[12] Finally, in 1978 Dick completed an entirely new work that drew upon the same autobiographical material as did the earlier novel. That was the book that was published in 1982 as *VALIS*.

In *Radio Free Albemuth* Philip K. Dick the science-fiction writer is a character from whose point of view much of the action is seen. He has a detached, sympathetic, but rather skeptical perspective on the strange experiences of his friend Nicholas Brady—who, like the real-life Dick, dropped out of school at Berkeley because of difficulties with ROTC; worked in a record store; saw a pink light in 1974 that gave him information that saved the life of his son. Brady also receives communications from an extraterrestrial source called Valis and feels his body taken over by another being, perhaps an early Christian returning to life. For the purposes of building a story based on incidents from his life, Dick seems to need to split himself in two. The writer persona stands back objectively to observe and record the mystical experiences and emotional traumas of the other more "subjective" and unreliable side of himself. Thus he transforms the raw experience into a form that gives it sense and order, tied to a coherent philosophical worldview.

Autobiography is basis for the plot, but Dick quickly veers into fiction. The whole novel, in fact, is set in an alternate universe in which a certain Ferris F. Fremont, rather than Richard Nixon, was elected president in 1978. The two are not dissimilar, but Nixon's paranoia about domestic "enemies" becomes Fremont's all-out campaign against a supposed conspiracy known as Aramchek. To crack down on this enemy, an insidious secret police organization called FAP (Friends of the American People) is set up. Both Brady and Dick (the character) quickly become targets of its harassment and are almost coerced into informing on each other's "subversive" activities. If Nicholas Brady is an alter ego of Philip K. Dick, at least they manage to avoid the situation of *A Scanner Darkly,* whose Bob Arctor is led to spy

on himself, and thus to become genuinely schizophrenic. In *VALIS,*
however, the presence of Dick's alter ego as a character will betoken a
psychotically split personality.

The first part of the book is told from the Dick character's point of
view; in the second, where Nicholas is the narrator, the visionary experiences predominate. A Roman sibyl speaks through Nicholas to al-
lay the FAPer's suspicions against him. That voice turns out to be
identical to Valis's (short for Vast Active Living Intelligence System),
which emanates from the distant star Albemuth via an alien satellite
in orbit around Earth. Due to the occluding influence of Valis's eternal
adversary, "Earth was still an unlit button on the exchange board of
the intergalactic communications network" (chap. 17). Valis, although
an AI (artificial intelligence) voice, is God, and its project none other
than to restore contact with the human race, which had "fallen" out of
touch. The nonhuman predecessors of Valis may be seen as such pre-
ternaturally wise machines as the talking taxicab in *Now Wait for Last
Year* or godlike aliens such as the Glimmung in *Galactic Pot-Healer.*
Valis is both artificial and living; it is pure consciousness, transcending
all boundaries, manifesting as an indescribable Other.

Nicholas identifies Valis with several traditional images of God: the
vegetation deity, the Corn King; the yang/yin polarity of active male
creator and receptive female shaper; the Judaeo-Christian God the Father. When Valis reveals itself to Nicholas as his father, however, it
goes beyond the traditional Christian implications. Valis's purpose is
to instruct him as to who he really is, which is "everyone" (chap. 23).
That is, Valis, Nicholas, and everyone else in the world are one cosmic
being. All of humanity are fragments of an original unfallen self. Valis
is perceived as external, extraterrestrial, but the stars are the reflection
of the inner state of man, and inner and outer are one. The absolute
object, the otherworldly voice that knows no conditions, is identical
with the absolute subject, the seed consciousness.

Ferris Fremont personifies the ignorance of the mass of people. He
gains power by preying on people's fear of the Soviets and of "the enemy within." This serves as convenient cover for his own conspiracies,
for he is behind the assassinations of major political figures—the Kennedys and Martin Luther King—and is in league with intelligence
agencies of both the U.S. and Soviet governments. FAP, his creation,
is a successor to Morec in *The Man Who Japed* and a precursor of the
Moral Majority. Actually, Fremont's obsession with Aramchek is not
merely paranoid. Through a young woman named Sadassa Silvia, born

Sadassa Aramchek, Nicholas learns that the conspiracy is real. Aramchek is the satellite that is beaming information to several thousand highly aware individuals around the world, forming a "collective brain." Through Aramchek, Nicholas and Sadassa are instructed to put out subliminal messages on popular records to convey the truth about the Fremont-Soviet connection; but FAP learns of the plot and arrests and kills them with disheartening suddenness. In a coda, however, narrated by Dick, who has been sentenced to hard labor, we learn that their sacrifice is not in vain, and that they have played a part in Valis's eventual victory. Furthermore, they have been granted immortality of the spirit through a "silver egg" that has been planted in them.

As a novel, *Radio Free Albemuth* is cast in a more straightforward science-fictional mode than the unconventional *Valis*. Also, its political theme and atmosphere of plots and conspiracies are much stronger than in the later novel. It may be that, with *VALIS*, Dick found the ideal vehicle for the cosmic scope of his vision—it was too big to be contained in a mere science-fiction novel, and he had to go on and invent something entirely new for it. But on it own merits, *Radio Free Albemuth* is an absorbing novel that is the best possible introduction to the material and preoccupations of Dick's later years.

## *VALIS*

*VALIS* is destined to remain Dick's most controversial novel. In it the author steps outside the conventions of fiction to inform the reader that he, Philip K. Dick, has had visionary experiences, information beamed directly into his brain from a godlike extraterrestrial entity named VALIS. But he does so in such a way as to distance himself from the revelation. Phil Dick the science-fiction writer is again a character, as he was in *Radio Free Albemuth*, but in *VALIS* his dreaming, visionary alter ego, Horselover Fat, is another side of Dick's psychotically split personality. Fat experiences many of the same events that Nicholas Brady does in the earlier novel. But here the Phil Dick narrator states at the outset: "I am Horselover Fat, and I am writing this in the third person to gain much-needed objectivity." When, however, much later in the novel, autobiography changes to science fiction and Fat is healed by the divine child Sophia, he "remembers" his true identity as Phil Dick, and Fat is incorporated and reintegrated in Phil's personality. Thus, as a rule, only when the subject matter is fact is the narrator insane; when he is sane, or whole, the book turns into fiction—which may be a way of saying that only an insane person would consider reality as anything other than a fiction.

Fat keeps a journal, the "Exegesis," in which he theorizes that we are all parts of a cosmic brain; everything, including ourselves, is information in this brain. And it is possible to contact the basis of that underlying unity of consciousness. He believes that the universe is an illusion but that God (or VALIS, or Zebra) is giving him glimpses of reality in the form of holograms produced by a beam of pink light aimed at his brain.

But the cosmic mind is deranged; there is a streak of irrationality in it. "Therefore someone in touch with reality is, by definition, in touch with the insane. . . . The only difference between us and Horselover Fat is that Fat knows his situation and we do not; therefore Fat is insane and we are normal" (chap. 3). The catch is that we are normal only by virtue of our ignorance of reality. But then normal Western society has always labeled its saints madmen.

Fat's vision of the "measureless void" (which corresponds to Dick's own experience of March 1974) is a genuine religious ecstasy. He perceives the infinite dimension of space, hears the cosmic hum, and feels the boundless love of the void (chap. 4). He reads the Gnostic gospels, which confirm his sense of an occluded, blind creator who opposes the rational true God, VALIS. In a sense, both are aspects of God, but the creator is impaired and has created the imperfect world that we inhabit. "The Empire never ended," Fat repeats: in some sense, we are still living in the Black Iron Prison of Roman Empire. The Logos, or "plasmate" (the blood plasma in the Holy Grail), is the countering principle to the insanity of the creator. VALIS cross-bonds selected human beings with the plasmate to create homoplasmates—those who are awakened to their infinite, divine inner selves.

The invasion of the universe by the Logos is a true communion, unlike the ghastly transubstantiation of the world into the body of the demonic creator, as in *The Three Stigmata of Palmer Eldritch*. But rather than man devouring God, God is devouring man and everything else: "The entire universe, possibly, is in the invisible process of turning into the Lord. And with this process comes not just sentience but— sanity" (chap. 5). Sanity here implies the ability to perceive reality, which is not merely relative and subjective: "Reality is that which, when we stop believing in it, it doesn't go away" (chap. 5). Fat's faith is not based on belief, but on experience—which is admittedly open to multiple interpretations, but undeniably reinforces his intuition that what we ordinarily see, touch, hear, taste, and smell is not all there is, and may not even be there at all.

Little actually happens for the first two-thirds of *VALIS*, making it for many a difficult novel to get through. Most of the attention is on Fat's visions and ideas, with long stretches of philosophy and quotations from the "Exegesis." The intellectual apparatus included to comment upon Fat's visions is almost mind-numbing, but it makes artistic sense. Without it, the reader would not give these experiences the credibility the author intends: they are made to tie in with the full range of religious and philosophical tradition extending back for thousand of years. Anyone attempting to dismiss Horselover Fat will also have to dismiss Parmenides, Heraclitus, Asklepios, Hermes Trismegistos, Plato, Lao-tzu, the Buddhist idealists, the Nag Hammadi gospels, Dante, Spinoza, Goethe, and many others. Dick takes Fat's experiences seriously—after all they are his own—and he wants us to do the same.

The first part of the novel does contain accounts of Fat's relationships with two women, Gloria and Sherri. The first kills herself, motivating Fat to a suicide attempt. The second, although in remission from cancer, fatalistically believes she will die anyway, and eventually does. Both women are self-destructive, and their doom poisons Fat by way of his sympathetic instincts. Saving people can be hazardous to your health: for Fat's sexual and emotional needs are as strong as his God-intoxication. And twentieth-century man does not live on manna alone.

The "story" really only begins in chapter 9, when Fat and his friends go to a film entitled *Valis*, whose plot and characters resemble that of *Radio Free Albemuth*. *Valis* the film serves a similar purpose to *VALIS* the novel as *The Grasshopper Lies Heavy* does to *The Man in the High Castle*. The worlds portrayed in both works-within-the-works resemble our own, but with odd incongruities. They are obviously fictions, but ones representing alternative realities that may have as much ontological substance as our own. The film seems to validate Fat's apparently insane reality in the eyes of his friends: David, a believing Catholic; Kevin, a skeptic and cynic; and "Phil," who of course is Fat himself. The four (or three) form the Rhipidon Society, and from here the science-fictional part of the story finally begins.

The friends contact Eric and Linda Lampton, the makers of the film, who claim to belong to the "Friends of God," a secret society dating back to Meister Eckehart, Ikhnaton, the Cyclops, and even Shiva himself. They also claim to be from a distant star, Albemuth. Linda's immaculately conceived daughter, Sophia, is supposedly the Savior. All this is a bit too much even for Fat to swallow; evidently prolonged exposure to the information beam of VALIS has fried the Lamptons' brains. They have been taken over by the god in a Dionysian possession, an "enthousiasmos." However, Sophia does seem to be authentically supernatural; a two-year-old child, she talks with complete lucidity and compelling authority.

When Fat meets Sophia, who is a dark-haired girl, appropriately enough, though a bit on the young side, she instantly reintegrates him with his proper self. Then she delivers his kerygma, or divine word: man is god, man is holy. She charges the Rhipidon Society with the goal of spreading this word to everybody. The Lamptons represent the desire to keep the truth restricted to an elite few. They are insane.

After the healed Phil Dick returns with his friends to Southern California, they receive word that Sophia has died. This disheartening news plunges Phil into bitterness and causes Fat to come out again and renew his spiritual quest with a new fervor. At the end, Fat is visiting ancient holy places around the world, while Phil waits at home in front of his television, seeking clues to the presence of VALIS in the "accidental" overlapping juxtaposition of commercials: "the symbols of the divine show up in our world initially at the trash stratum" (chap. 14). Illusion is whatever we expect to see; therefore, reality by definition is found wherever we least expect it.

The character Phil Dick, although a science-fiction writer, is less adventurous than Fat: he doesn't really want to break any new philosophical ground. Phil/Fat's wound was only temporarily healed—but that was preferable to being driven insane like the Lamptons. The revisioning process, the initiation into reality, must proceed at a gradual pace. Dick seems to fear, throughout his work, dissolving the illusion of maya too cataclysmically, whether through drugs, madness, divine revelation, or any other method. That is why in VALIS he keeps a piece of himself from being swept away with enthusiasm for the vision. He keeps his distance, and this gives the ending a downbeat tone that seems pessimistic to some. But it is significant that Phil, in front of his television, is hopeful that VALIS will return.

One critic has called Dick's gnosticism "ironic" because doubt is thrown on Horselover Fat's experiences by the narrator.[13] This is missing the point. Gnosticism is inherently ironic; it doubts everything. The distancing device of the narrator Dick uses is a way of defusing the reader's innate skepticism and drawing him inexorably, if not into belief, into a suspension of disbelief. In a letter Dick stated that *VALIS* "not only contains but *is premised upon* the kind of logical puzzle-problems-insights-doorways that Hofstadter deals with in his extraordinary book."[14] Dick had not read *Godel, Escher, Bach* at the time he wrote *VALIS,* but his novel perfectly fits the paradoxical "strange loop" form described by Hofstadter. Dick proceeds to explain his logic: all novels are falsehoods; *VALIS* is a novel and therefore false. Within the novel it is asserted that Horselover Fat only imagines he saw Christ. But "the disclaimer is unnecessary. (Since in a novel all assertions are axiomatically false.)" Thus Horselover Fat is sane; he actually did see Christ, and *VALIS* is not a novel (i.e., a falsehood). "The quintessential point is that *VALIS* is not a novel, Horselover Fat is not insane, I am not Horselover Fat." The assertion in the novel that he is Horselover Fat is untrue:

*Parts*—but only parts—of *VALIS* are true. *VALIS,* then, is a new kind of thing never seen before; it is neither novel nor autobiography, neither true nor false. It is a closed system with a regress built into it, a vicious (i.e., infinite) regress of which the author is aware (hence the disclaimer "Horselover Fat is insane"). Thus (and this, I think, is the *real* topic of *VALIS*) insanity (mental pathology) *is examined from inside.* The mind involved, (mine, presumably) is examining itself; it is thinking about its own thinking . . . Thinking, then, can only be veridical when it examines itself. Everything else is speculation and dubitable. Hence *VALIS* is important as a study of reality and how we know and what we know. It defines the limits and it states the situation.[15]

And, further, it reflects its content in its very form. It is as paradoxical a reality in itself as the paradoxical reality it contains.

*VALIS* is not a "metafiction" in the sense that it is self-reflexive, or aware of itself as a fiction. One might expect that having the author explicitly identified as the narrator, with his autobiography as a basis for the story, and mixing up fact, vision, dream, and fantasy, this could be nothing other than a metafiction. But it transcends even that transcendental category. Dick has tried neither to subvert the novel form nor to convert the reader to his vision. Rather he has created a literary artifact that is independent of both author and reader, complete in itself. More than any of Dick's other novels, it stretches fictional conventions to give the reader a virtually inexhaustible text that will simultaneously support and deny any interpretation. Time will prove it a Chinese finger-trap for critics.

## The Divine Invasion

Although it has no direct connection with *VALIS*, *The Divine Invasion*, written in 1980 and published in 1981, was originally titled *Valis Regained*. Certainly *VALIS* ends on a note of uncertainty, of a paradise lost, and in the later novel, though with different characters in different circumstances, the paradise is regained.

As in *VALIS*, Dick reverses his earlier theme of invasion by a destructive force (in *Palmer Eldritch* and others). Now the invader is God. The world belongs to Satan (here, Belial); God (Yah), projecting himself into the world in order to redeem it, has limited power and is born as a brain-damaged child, Emmanuel. Dick posits Yah as the basis of all existences. The cosmos is fragmented: there are different realities and Yah is himself part of that fragmentation. He is the source of evil as well as good, being the creator of darkness, as in a Bible verse that is quoted in the novel:

> I am the LORD, there is no other;
> I make the light, I create darkness,
> author alike of prosperity and trouble.
> I, the LORD, do all these things. (Isaiah, chap. 45)

Yah inflicts Job-like suffering on Rybys Romney, Emmanuel's mother. But by "falling" (in a sense he does this by incarnating as Emmanuel and his female counterpart, Zina), the god is humanized.

The relationship of the Upper Realm of Yah to the Lower Realm of Belial parallels the scheme of David Lindsay's classic *A Voyage to Arcturus* (1920). In that novel Crystalman, an evil power who masquerades as God, entraps the sparks of light emanating from the real Godhead, Surtur. These sparks are enslaved and become individual souls struggling for survival in the lower realm, Crystalman's world. This Gnostic formulation is reflected in Emmanuel's vision of "the Lower World— not as a place—but as transparent pictures permutating at immense velocity. These pictures were the Forms outside of space being fed into the Lower Realm to become reality" (chap. 5). Emmanuel, having penetrated the illusoriness of the mundane world, perceives the outline of the external world delineated in his own cosmic brain. He swallows the outer world: "He now had the universe inside him and his own brain outside everywhere . . . and because he had incorporated the world, he knew it *and controlled it*" (chap. 5). Though a god is doing this, the process applies to man as well. We all create the world in our consciousness and have the ability to change outer reality by operating on the inner level. Dick quotes Heraclitus to the effect that the microcosm and macrocosm are interlinked: "The truth is that what is above is like what is below and what is below is like what is above, to accomplish the miracles of the one thing" (chap. 5). This is perhaps the only novel in which Dick shows the universal orderliness underlying the material world. Instead of the malevolent influence of an individual consciousness on outer reality, whether it be Palmer Eldritch's, Jory's, or Alys Buckman's, we see instead gods with unfathomable wisdom recreating and refining the universe.

The fragmentation of the godhead has led to trouble. Part is transcendent (Yah) and part has fallen into the world as Emmanuel, Zina, and Belial. When Emmanuel takes on the unmerciful, judging personality of the transcendent Old Testament God, Zina teaches him to love the world by showing him her version of it. She makes him see the dignity of a dying dog, and realize that there can be no greater tragedy. She reminds him that, after all, evil was *his* creation, and she lifts his motives beyond the destruction of his adversary to love of mankind. By becoming aware of his oneness with Zina, he is able to defeat Belial, whose power only derives from the derangement of God.

Zina is identified with the Torah, which is not merely a scripture but the living blueprint of creation, according to the Judaic esotericism that permeates this novel. Reality alters according to how that blueprint is read; each individual in every age structures it anew. But there is one "primal or matrix Torah" underlying the changes (chap. 8), the giant computer program of the universe, with God the computer, the Vast Active Living Intelligence System.

Emmanuel and Zina, as male and female aspects of the godhead (En Sof and Shekhina, in Kabbalistic terminology), try to restructure the reality of Herb Asher, a typical Dickean little guy whom Yah plucks from a safe but useless existence in a dome on a distant planet to accompany Rybys to Earth as Emmanuel's legal father. Herb is almost killed in an accident and ends up in cryonic suspension for years, then is finally revived, only to be plunged into different versions of reality: Zina's, Emmanuel's, and Belial's. Reality is not fixed, but the one he gets to stay in is the one in which Herb makes a leap of cognition toward the highest degree of truth. He attains his fantasy of having a relationship with his ideal woman, the singer Linda Fox (who resembles Linda Ronstadt, except that she sings pop versions of John Dowland). He has the maturity to love her in the flesh as well as in the idealized image on holographic posters, despite his surprise that, like other real women, she menstruates. This sort of "disappointment" makes her more authentic and substantial.

Herb is allowed to unite with his anima, the woman of his dreams, and keep her, for Linda turns out to be his "Beside Helper." Every man has to choose between the Beside Helper and Belial; since Herb chooses the good, evil is defeated. It is a conscious decision on his part: he is not merely being pushed around by cosmic forces. He spontaneously fulfills what Emmanuel calls "the real law of life: mutual protection" (chap. 20). Herb will protect her where she is weak, even as she protects him. Dick's little man is victorious here as never before.

*The Divine Invasion* clearly fits the category of science fiction, unlike its predecessors *A Scanner Darkly* and *VALIS,* which are marginal science fiction. But Dick departs from conventional science fiction in assuming the utter reality of what religion describes, while staying within the scientific spirit of the quest for objectively verifiable knowledge. He continually alludes to religious and philosophical ideas of great profundity and historical resonance, while through the very structure of the narrative he emphasizes the relativity of time. The initial events of the story are remembered by Herb Asher as he lies in cryonic suspension, during which he also has a precognition of the time when he will be out of cryonic suspension. Herb doesn't know exactly when anything is actually happening, and neither do we. Is his experience live or on tape? The answer is that there is no true version of creation. Time is a conception to measure the infinite, which is continually re-creating itself within every moment. This is a wise book, permeated by knowledge and compassion, that opens new vistas in speculative fiction.

## The Transmigration of Timothy Archer

Dick's last novel, *The Transmigration of Timothy Archer,* was completed in June 1981 and published posthumously the following year. It is one of his finest achievements, and a triumphant return to realistic, mainstream writing, albeit with fantastic elements. Many fascinating conversations on philosophy, theology, and literature become the central focus of the book, as opposed to diversions from the plot. The play of ideas is compelling because it emanates from the life-and-death concerns of the characters, whose believability and humanity are perhaps greater than anywhere in Dick's writing.

The book is loosely based on the life of Episcopal Bishop James A. Pike, whom Dick knew. Like Pike, Timothy Archer is a seeker for truth who questions the Church's doctrine in favor of a direct revelation. Angel Archer—not based on a real person—is the narrator of the story. She is Archer's daughter-in-law, formerly married to Archer's son Jeff, who, like Pike's son, committed suicide. Archer's mistress Kirsten, who kills herself to end her suffering from a fatal cancer, corresponds with the stepmother of Nancy Hackett, Dick's fourth wife. The stepmother was Pike's mistress, and she also committed suicide.

A gifted, abstract philosophical and ethical thinker, Archer paradoxically becomes embroiled in the occult when all manner of table-tappings and stopped clocks are taken as signals from Jeff and evidence of an afterlife—and maybe they are, for the novel gives us no certainty on the matter. But the reality of the occult is not the issue: it is what attitude, idealistic or realistic, one should take toward life. Angel deplores Archer's readiness to disregard the consequences to his career and the necessity of keeping one's feet on the ground, in touch with the familiar and the concrete, as she is. He is like Horselover Fat, full of crazy ideas: he becomes convinced that a magic mushroom growing in the Holy Land was the source of the *anokhi,* or pure consciousness of God, which inspired the origin of Christianity. As happened to Pike, the impractical Archer's car breaks down in an Israeli desert, and he dies.

Yet Archer is a genuinely good man, even if his idealism is shown as inferior in many aspects, despite his erudition, to Angel's skeptical, worldly wisdom. She admires his moral stature: he is a man of peace, a friend of Martin Luther King and the Kennedys—but he does not have his feet on the ground. But when he asks her to accompany him to Israel, she refuses, choosing the "immediate, fixed, real, tangible" in the form of her home and job over the quest for the ultimate abstraction, the *anokhi.* She thereby makes "an incredible mistake," Dick stated in an interview.[16] If she had gone, Archer would not have driven into the desert without provisions, and would have survived. Confronted on all sides by the deaths of loved ones, Angel retreats completely into her shell. It is as if her soul dies and she becomes a machine (chap. 13).

Her mood is not improved when she finds that Archer's soul has apparently transmigrated to the body of Bill, Kirsten's mentally ill son, a person whose inability to understand abstract concepts makes him the unlikeliest possible vehicle. Even though Bill spouts Greek and other languages that he doesn't know, Angel refuses to accept occult explanations for these phenomena. She thinks it is only the concept, not the reality, of Timothy Archer that has come back to nest in Bill's deranged mind. Bill/Archer claims he found the *anokhi* in the desert—not the mushroom (which was just a crackpot theory, and a literalization of the idea of unbounded God-consciousness), but "the Presence" Itself (chap. 15). Experience of God has taken the place of theorizing. As to the truth of whether or not Timothy Archer has actually been reborn, Dick leaves the matter open. In an ordinary realistic fiction Angel's skepticism would represent the reference point of sanity and objective reality, but in any Dick novel, all bets are off. It can be read either way: the literal fact of Archer's reappearance (as of Sophia's divinity in *VALIS*) is unimportant. It is what you make of the situation, how humanly you can respond to it, that counts.

Despite her disillusionment and Berkeley-bred cynicism, Angel attends a seminar by a local Sufi guru, Edgar Barefoot. Unexpectedly, she finds herself softening and her intellectual armor melting away. Barefoot says that we both create the world and perceive it—a Phil Dick-like statement—and shows her the possibility of re-creating and forgiving herself. He frees her from self-absorption so she can turn her attention to another—in this case, Bill, whom she agrees to take into her home and care for. She realizes that if Archer's spirit does not live authentically in Bill, it does, somehow, in Barefoot, in his ability to save lives and guide people in a positive direction.

Dick had planned to write another science-fiction novel, *The Owl in Daylight,* based on Dante's *Divine Comedy*. It clearly would have been a further exploration of the universal and ultimately optimistic theme of *The Divine Invasion*: the transcendence of Inferno's Black Iron Prison in the experience of the paradisiacal "Palm Tree Garden."[17] He never lived to write it: *Timothy Archer* remains his last testament. After many flights of the imagination, he returned to Earth. It is perhaps fitting that the commonsensical Angel Archer is his last spokesperson: she is someone who stays up all night reading Dante in the midst of pain from an abscessed tooth. She concludes it is *all* real, the full range of experience from Inferno to Paradiso: "God save me from another night like that. But goddamn it, had I not lived out that night, drinking and crying and reading and hurting, I would never have been born, truly born. That was the time of my birth into the real world; and the real world, for me, is a mixture of pain and beauty, and this is the correct view of it because these are the components that make up reality" (chap. 9). Despite her lack of belief in Christianity, she is a religious person. Her name indicates her status. She cares, she loves, she feels. Dick's feminine side speaks at last, in the first person, and like Molly Bloom at the end of *Ulysses,* she strikes a life-affirming note, one grounded in earthly reality. Dick's quest comes to completion: he achieves an integration of the opposites of male and female, light and darkness, heaven and earth, peace and passion.

# Chapter Seven
# Toward the Future
## The Unity amidst Diversity

Dick was the master of the complex plot and multifocal narration. In his own thinking he seemed able to entertain simultaneously conflicting ideas. While working in a genre that places a premium on portraying change in the status quo, he speculated in areas that challenged and perplexed even those in the science-fiction community. His ideas burst boundaries; he focused on conveying the truth of his many-faceted vision without regard for critical expectations and genre conventions. It might seem that he was the complete relativist, almost a solipsist, denying the validity of any reality outside his own mind.

Dick himself looked for and found an overall thematic coherence in his work that transcended his personal concerns and addressed the ultimate questions of existence:

At one time my theme was the search for reality, which I posed as: What is real? What isn't? But I think really my theme, What is human? What isn't? is more vital and was there all the time underlying the other. After all, the subdivision of reality most important to our ability to make something we can treasure out of our life is the reality of other humans. To define what is real is to define what is human, if you care about humans.[1]

The imaginative structures Dick developed to carry the weight of this idea were often recycled, so that the main features of his world become instantly recognizable from novel to novel—one of corporate capitalism run amuck, totalitarian governments with psi police, depersonalized living in conapts, talking appliances, telepathic aliens with godlike powers, reality-altering drugs, and in the midst of it all ordinary men and women struggling to coexist with each other in the eternal battle of the sexes. The more irreal their world becomes, the more the *human* problem of how to learn to live with each other is thrown into relief.

Dick writes from a male perspective with no apologies. Women in his work are frequently archetypal, bitches or goddesses and frequently

128

both at once. The dark-haired girl as anima figure plays an almost obsessive role in catalyzing the Dickean hero into self-transformation. There is a subtle link between the recurrent anima character and Dick's visionary goals that reached their apogee in the Valis years. In his essay "The Evolution of a Vital Love" (1975) Dick wrote that the dark-haired girl had become for him the emblem of the authentic person as opposed to the android. He became less prone to portray these anima as contaminated by inhuman qualities, eaten up by bitchiness. In his later books sympathetic female characters include Donna in *A Scanner Darkly*, Sadassa in *Radio Free Albemuth*, Zina in *The Divine Invasion*, and Angel in *The Transmigration of Timothy Archer*. They came to represent an avenue of redemption through which Wisdom (allegorically suggested by Sophia in *VALIS*) could enlighten the Dickian hero struggling out of his occlusion.

The psychological concern with the hearts of men and women is really at the core of Dick's agenda as a science-fiction writer. The most radical concept in his speculative fiction is that consciousness and matter are one (though modern physics is near to embracing this Vedantist idea); by penetrating the world's maya we realize our true, unfallen, human divinity. In that process the woman upon whom a man projects his anima is revisioned in her universal aspect—neither as a goddess nor a bitch, but a human being capable of giving and receiving love, like Linda Fox in *The Divine Invasion*. In fact, for Dick she is the channel through which the world is revisioned and the bars of the Black Iron Prison are lifted.

## Dick's Legacy

Although there is nothing like universal agreement on what Dick's best novels are, certain titles recur on most people's lists: *The Man in the High Castle, Martian Time-Slip, The Three Stigmata of Palmer Eldritch, Dr. Bloodmoney, Do Androids Dream of Electric Sheep?, Ubik.* Opinion on *VALIS* is split: some think it his masterpiece, others find it unreadable. The 1950s novels, particularly *Eye in the Sky* and *Time Out of Joint*, have their adherents. *Flow My Tears, the Policeman Said* is a strong novel, as is *A Scanner Darkly*. Ursula Le Guin favors *The Transmigration of Timothy Archer* and has a special fondness for *Galactic Pot-Healer*. Biographer Gregg Rickman's favorite Dick novel is *Counter-Clock World*. Paul Williams ranks *Confessions of a Crap Artist* with Dick's best; the recent publication of most of the other mainstream novels has aroused serious attention and often admiration. And what of the raft of 1960s novels that tend to be overlooked, but for many readers yield considerable pleasures: for example, *The Simulacra, Now Wait for Last Year, The Game-Players of Titan, The Zap Gun, We Can Build You?* Then there are the short stories, recently collected in five volumes, many of which are classics. In short, too much of Dick is good to reduce his contribution to one or even a few titles. He was and is a phenomenon.

One's evaluation of Philip K. Dick as a major twentieth-century author depends on what one thinks of science fiction in general and also on one's sympathy toward Dick's central concern with the nature of reality. Clearly, he never attempted to disown the science-fiction genre. Dick's fiction is crammed with the familiar science-fiction motifs—space and time travel, dystopian societies, post-holocaust futures, other planets, aliens, robots and androids, psi powers, and altered states of consciousness. He generally uses all of these in highly original ways, but at least until the Valis novels, he gloried in this standard repertoire of science-fiction images and plot elements. Dick was completely at home in the science-fiction world; his whole approach to his art was in terms of speculation, and conventional realistic fiction could not contain his ideas.

Because of the structure by which publishers package their product, genre labels are convenient and it is often difficult for a genre author to obtain recognition outside his field. Sometimes a science-fiction writer will break away and achieve best-seller status (Robert A. Heinlein, Frank Herbert), and less frequently literary acclaim (Ursula Le Guin, Stanislaw Lem). Dick did neither. He continues to have a respectably large reading audience, especially when taking into account fans in foreign countries like France, where he is quite popular: but in his lifetime he never enjoyed the universal acclaim many feel he deserved, and may yet achieve.

Academics and scholars who write about science fiction have paid more attention to Dick than to perhaps any other contemporary science-fiction writer, but on the whole academia retains its habitual prejudice against science fiction as a serious literary expression. Thus it may take some years before such inbred snobbery dissipates and Dick, along with science-fiction writers in general, can receive their due.

The radicalism of Dick's speculative approach causes him to transcend thoroughly the conventions of the science-fiction genre. To be appreciated fully, he requires a readership ready to have its boundaries stretched beyond the limit. He wrote metaphysical fiction, in which the *starting point* was the already bizarre future world he developed with science-fiction motifs. From there, he plunged into paradox. He tied the minds of his characters in knots. He found humanity in the inhuman and vice versa. He exposed his characters to Absolute Good and Absolute Evil. He made philosophy concrete. He questioned the reality of reality. He arrived, finally, at the meta-metafiction of *VALIS,* which approaches religious revelation through a schizophrenic narrator disguised as the author.

Thus Dick presents intellectual challenges that are found in few other writers. Yet his style is never obfuscatory or pretentiously literary; it never calls attention to itself. The notion that *this world is not real,* a theme that permeates his works, may be inherently disturbing and confusing to some. But the confusion is not in the presentation of the idea: that is clear enough. In a way it is the simplest of ideas, and therefore the hardest to understand or accept.

It is not quite true that Dick believed that all reality was subjective, capable of dissolving with an unexpected shift in a person's consciousness. It does so often enough in his stories, but always in the context of a progression toward something unchanging and eternal. That sounds like religion, and Dick was a profoundly religious writer: but he had no faith in faith, and his answers were mostly questions.

What is so endearing about Dick is that along with this radical Gnostic transcendentalism he maintains a firm groundedness in ordinary reality and a sensitivity to the need for love in people's lives. Dick's characters are Everyman—nakedly vulnerable, imperfect, they are forced into situations where their worlds are turned upside down—and yet they exhibit courage and win their modest victories. They find moral paths amidst bewildering changes in their inner and outer realities.

In the twentieth century we have witnessed the most rapid technological growth in the history of humankind, as well as the most dramatic upheaval in human consciousness. As physics traces the basis of objective reality to the unified field, individuals throughout the world have quietly reshaped the world they live in by exploring their subjective realities and bringing forth new, creative ideas from the unified field therein. Dick reflects both of these evolutionary trends, outer and inner. Although he has stopped, his work has not. It keeps on growing in significance, influence, resonance, and recognition. As much as he wrote about the future, so may the future write about him.

# Notes and References

*Chapter One*

1. Paul Williams, *Only Apparently Real* (New York: Arbor House, 1986), 48.
2. *The Double: Bill Symposium,* ed. Bill Mallardi and Bill Bowers (Akron, Ohio: D:B Press, 1969), 70.
3. Ibid., 18.
4. Ibid., 52.
5. "Introduction" in *The Golden Man* (New York: Berkley, 1980), xvi.
6. Dick, quoted in *Dream Makers* by Charles Platt (New York: Berkley, 1980), 155.
7. Williams, *Only Apparently Real,* 50.

*Chapter Two*

1. *PKD: A Philip K. Dick Bibliography* by Daniel J. H. Levack (San Francisco and Columbia, Penn.: Underwood/Miller, 1981), 101.
2. Ibid., 99.
3. Ibid., 125.
4. See Mircea Eliade, *A History of Religious Ideas,* (Chicago: University of Chicago Press, 1978), 1:310.
5. Thomas M. Disch, "Toward the Transcendent: An Introduction to *Solar Lottery* and Other Works," in *Philip K. Dick,* ed. Martin Harry Greenberg and Joseph D. Olander (New York: Taplinger, 1983), 18.
6. "Afterword," in Levack, *PKD,* 154.
7. The order of composition for Dick's novels, which determines the sequence used in this study, is not definitely known in all cases. Paul Williams has compiled a useful list of the novels according to the dates they were received by Dick's agent, the Scott Meredith Literary Agency. See the Appendix in Williams's *Only Apparently Real,* 178–84.
8. *Philip K. Dick: In His Own Words* by Gregg Rickman (Long Beach: Fragments West/Valentine Press, 1984), 132.
9. "Letter of Comment," in *Philip K. Dick: Electric Shepherd,* ed. Bruce Gillespie (Melbourne: Norstrilia Press, 1975), 31–32.
10. Damon Knight, *In Search of Wonder,* 2d ed. (Chicago: Advent, 1967), 232.
11. Rickman, *In His Own Words,* 128.
12. Lou Stathis, "Afterword," *Time out of Joint* (New York: Bluejay, 1984), 258.

13. "Letter of Comment," in *Philip K. Dick: Electric Shepherd*, 32.

14. Rickman, *In His Own Words*, 138.

15. Stathis, "Afterword," 260.

16. Rickman, *In His Own Words*, 140.

*Chapter Three*

1. Rickman, *In His Own Words*, 147.

2. Kim Stanley Robinson, *The Novels of Philip K. Dick* (Ann Arbor: UMI Research Press, 1984), 3.

3. Paul Williams, "Introduction" in *Confessions of a Crap Artist* (Glen Ellen, Calif.: Entwhistle Books, 1975), ix.

4. Rickman, *In His Own Words*, 18.

5. *A Letter from Philip K. Dick: February 1, 1960* (Glen Ellen, Calif.: Philip K. Dick Society, 1983), 10.

*Chapter Four*

1. Ursula Le Guin, Letter, *Foundation*, no. 27 (February 1983), 108.

2. N. B. Hayles, "Metaphysics and Metafiction in *The Man in the High Castle*," in *Philip K. Dick*, ed. Greenberg and Olander, 67.

3. Joseph Milicia, "Introduction" in *The Man in the High Castle* (Boston: Gregg Press, 1979), xxxiv.

4. "Letter of Comment" in *Philip K. Dick: Electric Shepherd*, 32.

5. "Afterword" in Levack, *PKD*, 154.

6. Letter from Ted White, *Philip K. Dick Society Newsletter*, no. 6 (April 1985), 8.

7. Robinson, *Novels of PKD*, 135.

8. Rickman, *In His Own Words*, 157.

9. R. D. Laing, *The Politics of Experience* (New York: Ballantine, 1967), 129, 126.

10. Fredric Jameson, "After Armageddon: Character Systems in *Dr. Bloodmoney*," *Science-Fiction Studies* 2 (March 1975): 42.

11. "Afterword," in *Dr. Bloodmoney* (New York: Bluejay, 1985), 302.

12. Ibid., 301.

13. Robinson, *Novels of PKD*, 79.

14. Rickman, *In His Own Words*, 154.

15. D. Scott Apel and Kevin Briggs, "An Interview with Philip K. Dick," *Philip K. Dick Society Newsletter*, no. 6 (April 1985), 13.

16. Paul Williams, "Introduction" in *The Three Stigmata of Palmer Eldritch* (Boston: Gregg Press, 1979), vi.

*Chapter Five*

1. Dick, "The Missing Pages of *The Unteleported Man*," *Philip K. Dick Society Newsletter*, no. 8 (September 1985), 2, 13.

2. Ibid., 13.

3. Rickman, *In His Own Words,* 170.

4. Ibid., 252.

5. David G. Hartwell, "Introduction" in *Counter-Clock World* (Boston: Gregg Press, 1979), vii.

6. Rickman, *In His Own Words,* 171, 173–80.

7. Robinson, *Novels of PKD,* 87.

8. "Man, Android and Machine," in *Science Fiction at Large,* ed. Peter Nicholls (New York: Harper, 1976), 202–3.

9. Ibid., 215.

10. *Ubik: The Screenplay* (Minneapolis: Corroboree Press, 1985), x.

11. Michael Bishop, "In Pursuit of *Ubik,*" in *Philip K. Dick,* ed. Greenberg and Olander, 147.

12. Ian Watson, "Le Guin's *Lathe of Heaven* and the Role of Dick: The False Reality as Mediator," *Science-Fiction Studies* 2 (March 1975): 71.

13. Hazel Pierce, *Philip K. Dick* (Mercer Island, Wash.: Starmont House, 1982), 32.

14. Robinson, *Novels of PKD,* 97.

15. Peter Fitting, "*Ubik*: The Deconstruction of Bourgeois SF," in *Philip K. Dick,* ed. Greenberg and Olander, 155.

16. "Man, Android and Machine," 208.

17. *Ubik: The Screenplay,* x.

18. Ibid., 25.

19. David Bohm, *Wholeness and the Implicate Order* (London: Routledge & Kegan Paul, 1980), 134.

20. Paul Davies, *Superforce: The Search for a Grand Unified Theory of Nature* (New York: Simon & Schuster, 1984), 7.

21. Robinson, *Novels of PKD,* 104.

22. Rickman, *In His Own Words,* 183–84.

23. Williams, "Introduction" in *The Three Stigmata of Palmer Eldritch,* xvi.

24. Williams, *Only Apparently Real,* 183.

25. Rickman, *In His Own Words,* 190.

*Chapter Six*

1. "The Dark-Haired Girl," unpublished MS., Special Collections, California State University at Fullerton.

2. [Mike Hodel], "The Mainstream that Through the Ghetto Flows: An Interview with Philip K. Dick," *Missouri Review* 7,2 (1984): 175.

3. Platt, "Philip K. Dick," in *Dream Makers,* 149.

4. Rickman, *In His Own Words,* 190.

5. Ibid.

6. Dick, "Excerpts from the 'The Exegesis,' " *Gnosis,* no. 1 (Fall/Winter 1985), 15.

7. "The Exegesis," unpublished MS., Estate of Philip K. Dick.

8. "Excerpts," 13.

9. "The Exegesis."

10. "Excerpts," 13.

11. "The Exegesis."

12. See Williams, *Only Apparently Real*, 147–50, and "Mark Hurst/ Philip K. Dick Chronology," *Philip K. Dick Newsletter*, no. 12 (October 1986), 7.

13. Robert Galbreath, "Salvation-Knowledge: Ironic Gnosticism in *Valis* and *The Flight to Lucifer*," in *Science-Fiction Dialogues*, ed. Gary Wolfe (Chicago: Academy Chicago, 1982), 116.

14. Dick, "Was Horselover Fat a Flake?" *Philip K. Dick Society Newsletter*, no. 15 (August 1987), 5.

15. Ibid., 6.

16. Rickman, *In His Own Words*, 219.

17. Ibid., 254.

*Chapter Seven*

1. "The Evolution of a Vital Love," MS., Special Collections, California State University at Fullerton.

# Selected Bibliography

PRIMARY SOURCES

1. Novels
*Blade Runner.* (See *Do Androids Dream of Electric Sheep?*)
*The Broken Bubble.* New York: Arbor House, 1988.
*Clans of the Alphane Moon.* New York: Ace, 1964.
*Confessions of a Crap Artist.* Glen Ellen, Calif.: Entwhistle Books, 1975.
*The Cosmic Puppets.* New York: Ace, 1957.
*Counter-Clock World.* New York: Berkley, 1967.
*The Crack in Space.* New York: Ace, 1966.
*Deus Irae* (with Roger Zelazny). Garden City, N.Y.: Doubleday, 1976.
*The Divine Invasion.* New York: Simon & Schuster, 1981.
*Do Androids Dream of Electric Sheep?* Garden City, N.Y.: Doubleday, 1968. As
    *Blade Runner.* New York: Ballantine, 1982.
*Dr. Bloodmoney, or How We Got Along after the Bomb.* New York: Ace, 1965.
*Dr. Futurity.* New York: Ace, 1960.
*Eye in the Sky.* New York: Ace, 1957.
*Flow My Tears, the Policeman Said.* Garden City, N.Y.: Doubleday, 1974.
*Galactic Pot-Healer.* New York: Berkley, 1969.
*The Game-Players of Titan.* New York: Ace, 1963.
*The Ganymede Takeover* (with Ray Nelson). New York: Ace, 1967.
*Humpty Dumpty in Oakland.* London: Gollancz, 1986.
*In Milton Lumky Territory.* Pleasantville, N.Y.: Dragon Press, 1985.
*Lies, Inc.* (See *The Unteleported Man*).
*The Man in the High Castle.* New York: Putnam, 1962.
*The Man Who Japed.* New York: Ace, 1956.
*The Man Whose Teeth Were All Exactly Alike.* Willimantic, Conn.: Mark V.
    Ziesing, 1984.
*Martian Time-Slip.* New York: Ballantine, 1964.
*Mary and the Giant.* New York: Arbor House, 1987.
*A Maze of Death.* Garden City, N.Y.: Doubleday, 1970.
*Now Wait for Last Year.* Garden City, N.Y.: Doubleday, 1966.
*Our Friends from Frolix 8.* New York: Ace, 1970.
*The Penultimate Truth.* New York: Belmont, 1964.
*Puttering about in a Small Land.* Chicago: Academy Chicago, 1985.
*Radio Free Albemuth.* New York: Arbor House, 1985.
*A Scanner Darkly.* Garden City, N.Y.: Doubleday, 1977.

*The Simulacra.* New York: Ace, 1964.

*Solar Lottery.* New York: Ace, 1955. As *World of Chance* [alternate version]. London: Rich & Cowan, 1955.

*The Three Stigmata of Palmer Eldritch.* Garden City, N.Y.: Doubleday, 1965.

*Time out of Joint.* Philadelphia: Lippincott, 1959.

*The Transmigration of Timothy Archer.* New York: Timescape, 1982.

*Ubik.* Garden City, N.Y.: Doubleday, 1969.

*The Unteleported Man.* New York: Ace, 1966 (first version). New York: Berkley, 1983 (second version). As *Lies, Inc.* London: Gollancz, 1984 (third version).

*VALIS.* New York: Bantam, 1981.

*Vulcan's Hammer.* New York: Ace, 1960.

*We Can Build You.* New York: DAW, 1972.

*The World Jones Made.* New York: Ace, 1956.

*World of Chance.* (See *Solar Lottery*)

*The Zap Gun.* New York: Pyramid, 1967.


2. Collections

*The Best of Philip K. Dick.* Edited by John Brunner. New York: Ballantine, 1977.

*The Book of Philip K. Dick.* New York: DAW, 1973.

*The Collected Stories of Philip K. Dick.* 5 vols. San Francisco, Calif. and Columbia, Pa.: Underwood/Miller, 1987.

*The Golden Man.* Edited by Mark Hurst. New York: Berkley, 1980.

*A Handful of Darkness.* London: Rich & Cowan, 1955.

*I Hope I Shall Arrive Soon.* Edited by Mark Hurst and Paul Williams. New York: Doubleday, 1985.

*A Philip K. Dick Omnibus* [comprises *The Crack in Space, The Unteleported Man,* and *Dr. Futurity*]. London: Sidgwick & Jackson, 1970.

*The Preserving Machine.* New York: Ace, 1969.

*Robots, Androids, and Mechanical Oddities.* Edited by Patricia S. Warrick and Martin H. Greenberg. Carbondale and Edwardsville: Southern Illinois University Press, 1984.

*The Variable Man and Other Stories.* New York: Ace, 1957.


3. Short Fiction

"Adjustment Team." *Orbit Science Fiction,* September-October 1954.

"The Alien Mind." *Yuba City High Times,* 20 February 1981.

"Autofac." *Galaxy,* November 1955.

"Beyond Lies the Wub." *Planet Stories,* July 1952.

"Beyond the Door." *Fantastic Universe,* January 1954.

"Breakfast at Twilight." *Amazing,* July 1954.

"The Builder." *Amazing,* December 1953-January 1954.

"Cadbury, the Beaver Who Lacked." In *The Collected Stories of Philip K. Dick,* 1987. *See* Collections.

"Cantata 140." *Magazine of Fantasy and Science Fiction*, July 1964.

"Captive Market." *If*, April 1955.

"Chains of Air, Web of Aether." In *Stellar #5*, edited by Judy-Lynn del Rey. New York: Ballantine, 1980.

"The Chromium Fence." *Imagination*, July 1955.

"Colony." *Galaxy*. June 1953.

"The Commuter." *Amazing*, August-September 1953.

"The Cookie Lady." *Fantasy Fiction*, June 1953.

"The Cosmic Poachers." *Imagination*, July 1953.

"The Crawlers." *Imagination*, July 1954.

"The Crystal Crypt." *Planet Stories*, January 1954.

"The Day Mr. Computer Fell Out of Its Tree." In *The Collected Stories of Philip K. Dick*, 1987. *See* Collections.

"The Days of Perky Pat." *Amazing*, December 1963.

"The Defenders." *Galaxy*, January 1953.

"The Electric Ant." *Magazine of Fantasy and Science Fiction*, October 1969.

"Exhibit Piece." *If*, August 1954.

"The Exit Door Leads In." *Rolling Stone College Papers*, Fall 1979.

"Expendable." *Magazine of Fantasy and Science Fiction*, July 1953.

"Explorers We." *Magazine of Fantasy and Science Fiction*, January 1959.

"The Eyes Have It." *Science Fiction Stories*, no. 1 (1953).

"The Eye of the Sibyl." In *The Collected Stories of Philip K. Dick*, 1987. *See* Collections.

"Fair Game." *If*, September 1959.

"Faith of Our Fathers." In *Dangerous Visions*, edited by Harlan Ellison. Garden City, N.Y.: Doubleday, 1967.

"The Father-Thing." *Magazine of Fantasy and Science Fiction*, December 1954.

"Foster, You're Dead." In *Star Science Fiction Stories 3*, edited by Frederick Pohl. New York: Ballantine, 1955.

"Frozen Journey" [reprinted as "I Hope I Shall Arrive Soon"]. *Playboy*, December 1980.

"A Game of Unchance." *Amazing*, July 1964.

"The Golden Man." *If*, April 1954.

"The Great C." *Cosmos*, September 1953.

"The Gun." *Planet Stories*, September 1952.

"The Hanging Stranger." *Science Fiction Adventures*, December 1953.

"Holy Quarrel." *Worlds of Tomorrow*, May 1966.

"The Hood Maker." *Imagination*, June 1955.

"Human Is." *Startling Stories*, Winter 1955.

"If There Were No Benny Cemoli." *Galaxy*, December 1963.

"The Impossible Planet." *Imagination*, October 1953.

"Impostor." *Astounding*, June 1953.

"The Indefatigable Frog." *Fantastic Story Magazine*, July 1953.

"The Infinites." *Planet Stories*, May 1953.

"James P. Crow." *Planet Stories*, May 1954.

"Jon's World." In *Time to Come*, edited by August Derleth. New York: Farrar Straus & Young, 1954.
"The King of the Elves." *Beyond Fantasy Fiction*, September 1953.
"The Last of the Masters." *Orbit Science Fiction*, November-December 1954.
"The Little Black Box." *Worlds of Tomorrow*, August 1964.
"The Little Movement." *Magazine of Fantasy and Science Fiction*, November 1952.
"A Little Something for Us Tempunauts." In *Final Stage*, edited by Edward L. Ferman and Barry N. Malzberg. New York: Charterhouse, 1974.
"Martians Come in Clouds." *Fantastic Universe*, June-July 1954.
"Meddler." *Future*, October 1954.
"The Minority Report." *Fantastic Universe*, January 1956.
"Misadjustment." *Science Fiction Quarterly*, February 1957.
"The Mold of Yancy," *If*, August 1955.
"Mr. Spaceship." *Imagination*, January 1953.
"Nanny." *Startling Stories*, Spring 1955.
"Not By Its Cover." *Famous Science Fiction*, Summer 1968.
"Novelty Act." *Fantastic*, February 1964.
"Null-O." *If*, December 1958.
"Of Withered Apples." *Cosmos*, July 1954.
"Oh, To Be A Blobel!" *Galaxy*, February 1964.
"Orpheus with Clay Feet" [Jack Dowland, pseud.]. *Escapade*, c. 1964.
"Out in the Garden." *Fantasy Fiction*, August 1953.
"Pay for the Printer." *Satellite Science Fiction*, October 1956.
"Paycheck." *Imagination*, June 1953.
"Piper in the Woods." *Imagination*, February 1953.
"Planet for the Transients." *Fantastic Universe*, October-November 1953.
"Precious Artifact." *Galaxy*, October 1964.
"The Pre-Persons." *Magazine of Fantasy and Science Fiction*, October 1974.
"A Present for Pat." *Startling Stories*, January 1954.
"The Preserving Machine." *Magazine of Fantasy and Science Fiction*, June 1953.
"Prize Ship." *Thrilling Wonder Stories*, Winter 1954.
"Progeny." *If*, November 1954.
"Project: Earth." *Imagination*, December 1953.
"Prominent Author." *If*, May 1954.
"Psi-Man Heal My Child!" [reprinted as "Psi-Man"]. *Imaginative Tales*, November 1955.
"Rautavaara's Case." *Omni*, October 1980.
"Recall Mechanism." *If*, July 1959.
"Retreat Syndrome." *Worlds of Tomorrow*, January 1965.
"Return Match." *Galaxy*, February 1967.
"Roog." *Magazine of Fantasy and Science Fiction*, February 1953.
"Sales Pitch." *Future*, June 1954.
"Second Variety." Space Science Fiction, May 1953.

"Service Call." *Science Fiction Stories*, July 1955.

"Shell Game." *Galaxy*, September 1954.

"The Short Happy Life of the Brown Oxford." *Magazine of Fantasy and Science Fiction*, January 1954.

"The Skull." *If*, September 1952.

"Small Town." *Amazing*, May 1954.

"Some Kinds of Life" [Richard Phillipps, pseud.]. *Fantastic Universe*, October-November 1953.

"Souvenir." *Fantastic Universe*, October 1954.

"Stability." In *The Collected Stories of Philip K. Dick*, 1987. *See* Collections.

"Stand-By" [reprinted as "Top Stand-By Job"]. *Amazing*, October 1963.

"The Story to End All Stories for Harlan Ellison's Anthology *Dangerous Visions*." *Niekas*, Fall 1968.

"Strange Eden." *Imagination*, December 1954.

"Strange Memories of Death." *Interzone*, Summer 1984.

"A Surface Raid." *Fantastic Universe*, July 1955.

"Survey Team." *Fantastic Universe*, May 1954.

"A Terran Odyssey." In *The Collected Stories of Philip K. Dick*, 1987. *See* Collections.

"Time Pawn." *Thrilling Wonder Stories*, Summer 1954.

"To Serve the Master." *Imagination*, February 1956.

"Tony and the Beetles." In *Orbit Science Fiction*, no. 2 (1953).

"The Trouble with Bubbles." *If*, September 1953.

"The Turning Wheel." *Science Fiction Stories*, no. 2 (1954).

"The Unreconstructed M." *Science Fiction Stories*, January 1957.

"Upon the Dull Earth." *Beyond Fantasy Fiction*, November 1954.

"The Variable Man." *Space Science Fiction*, September 1953.

"Vulcan's Hammer." *Future*, no. 29 (1956).

"War Game." *Galaxy*, December 1959.

"War Veteran." *If*, March 1955.

"The War with the Fnools." *Galactic Outpost*, Spring 1964.

"Waterspider." *If*, January 1964.

"We Can Remember It for You Wholesale." *Magazine of Fantasy and Science Fiction*, April 1966.

"What the Dead Men Say." *Worlds of Tomorrow*, June 1964.

"What'll We Do With Ragland Park?" *Amazing*, November 1963.

"A World of Talent." *Galaxy*, October 1954.

"The World She Wanted." *Science Fiction Quarterly*, May 1953.

"Your Appointment Will Be Yesterday." *Amazing*, August 1966.


4. Non-Fiction

"Afterthoughts by the Author." In *The Best of Philip K. Dick*, edited by John Brunner, 443–50. New York: Ballantine, 1977.

"Afterword." In *Dr. Adder*, by K. W. Jeter, 228–31. New York: Bluejay Books, 1984.

"Afterword." In *Dr. Bloodmoney*, 299–304. New York: Bluejay Books, 1985.

"The Android and the Human." *SF Commentary*, no. 31 (December 1972), 4–26.

"Another Passion." *Niekas*, November 1981, 30–31.

"Anthony Boucher." *Magazine of Fantasy and Science Fiction*, August 1968.

"Drugs, Hallucinations, and the Quest for Reality." *Lighthouse*, no. 11 (November 1964).

"The Evolution of a Vital Love." Supplement to *Mike Bailey's Personalzine*, nos. 20–21 (1975).

"An Excerpt from the Exegesis." *Philip K. Dick Society Newsletter*, no. 12 (October 1986), 3–5.

"Excerpts from 'The Exegesis.' " *Gnosis*, no. 1 (Fall/Winter 1985), 12–15.

"His Predictions." In *The Book of Predictions*, 328–29. Edited by David Wallechinsky. New York: Morrow, 1980.

"How to Build a Universe That Doesn't Fall apart Two Days Later." In *I Hope I Shall Arrive Soon*, 1–23. *See* Collections.

"A Letter from Philip K. Dick." *Scintillation* 4 (March 1977); 17, 38–39.

*A Letter from Philip K. Dick: February 1, 1960*. Glen Ellen, Calif.: Philip K. Dick Society, 1983.

"Letter of Comment." *SF Commentary*, no. 9 (February 1970), 8–10, and *Philip K. Dick: Electric Shepherd*, edited by Bruce Gillespie, 31–33.

"Letter of Comment." *SF Commentary*, no. 17 (November 1970): 5–7, and *Philip K. Dick: Electric Shepherd*, edited by Bruce Gillespie, 44–45. Partially reprinted in *PKD: A Philip K. Dick Bibliography*, by Daniel J. H. Levack, 144–45. San Francisco: Underwood/Miller, 1981.

"The Lucky Dog Pet Store." *Foundation*, no. 17 (September 1979). Reprinted as "Now Wait for This Year" in *Philip K. Dick*, edited by Greenberg and Olander, 215–27, and in *The Golden Man*, edited by Mark Hurst, xv–xviii.

"Man, Android and Machine." In *Science Fiction at Large*, edited by Peter Nicholls, 202–24. New York: Harper, 1976.

"Memories Found in a Bill from a Small Animal Vet." *Real World*, no. 5 (February-March 1976), 4–5.

"My Definition of Science Fiction." *Just SF*, no. 1 (1981).

"Naziism and the High Castle." *Niekas*, no. 9 (September 1964).

"The Nixon Crowd." *SF Commentary*, no. 39 (November 1973).

"Notes Made Late at Night by a Weary SF Writer." *Eternity Science Fiction*, o.s., no. 1 (July 1972), 26.

"An Open Letter from Philip K. Dick." *Vertex* 2 (October 1974), 99.

"Preface." in *The Collected Stories of Philip K. Dick*, 1: xiii–xiv. *See* Collections.

"Schizophrenia and the Book of Changes." *Niekas*, no. 11 (March 1965).

"Scientists Claim: We Are Center of the Universe." *New Worlds,* no. 216 (September 1979).

"Self-Portrait." *PKDS Newsletter,* no. 2 (December 1983).

"The Short, Happy Life of a Science Fiction Writer." *Scintillation* 3, 3 (June 1976): 11–14.

"Story Notes" and "Afterword." In *The Golden Man,* edited by Mark Hurst, 332–37. *See* Collections.

"Thoughts on VALIS." *New Pathways,* no. 7 (April 1987), 15–16.

"[Unpublished] Foreword to *The Preserving Machine.*" *Science-Fiction Studies* 2 (March 1975): 22–23.

"Was Horselover Fat a Flake?" *Philip K. Dick Society Newsletter,* no. 15 (August 1987): 5–6.

"Will the Atomic Bomb Ever Be Perfected, and If So, What Becomes of Robert Heinlein?" *Lighthouse,* no. 14 (October 1966), 3–6.

"Who is An SF Writer?" In *Science Fiction: The Academic Awakening.* Edited by Willis E. McNelly, 46–50. Shreveport, La.: College English Association, 1974.


5. Other

"The Acts of Paul." With *The Collected Stories of Philip K. Dick,* slipcased edition. *See* Collections. Synopsis for novel.

"Fawn, Look Back." *Science Fiction Eye,* no. 2 (August 1987). Outline for novel.

"The Missing Pages of *The Unteleported Man.*" *Philip K. Dick Society Newsletter,* no. 8 (September 1985), 2, 13.

"My Life in Stillness: White as Day." *Last Wave,* no. 1 (October 1983), 26–27. Poem.

"On a Cat Which Fell Three Stories and Survived." *Last Wave,* no. 3 (Summer 1984), 29. Poem.

"Philip K. Dick Alone: Notes for Work-in Progress, Circa August 1974." *Philip K. Dick Society Newsletter,* no. 9/10. Sound recording. Notes for unwritten sequel to *The Man in the High Castle.*

*Ubik: The Screenplay.* Minneapolis, Minn.: Corroboree, 1985.

*Warning: We Are Your Police. PKDS Newsletter,* no. 7 (July 1985). Outline for television script.


6. Unpublished Materials

In Special Collections, California State University, Fullerton, Calif.:

"The Dark-Haired Girl." Series of letters, 1972.

"Gather Yourselves Together." Novel, mid-1950s.

"The Glimmung of Plowman's Planet." Children's novel, 1966.

"Voices from the Street." Novel, 1954.

In possession by the Estate of Philip K. Dick, Glen Ellen, Calif.: "Exegesis." Journal, 1974-82.

## SECONDARY SOURCES

### 1. Bibliography

Levack, Daniel J. H. *PKD: A Philip K. Dick Bibliography.* San Francisco, Calif., and Columbia, Pa.: Underwood/Miller, 1981. Illustrated, annotated listing of all editions of Dick's novels, stories, and articles, including translations.

### 2. Books

Apel, D. Scott, ed. *Philip K. Dick: The Dream Connection.* San Jose, Calif.: Permanent Press, 1987. Consists of a long interview with Dick, selected correspondence, and material about Dick by several other writers.

Gillespie, Bruce, ed. *Philip K. Dick: Electric Shepherd.* Melbourne, Australia: Nostrilia Press, 1975. Articles, reviews, and letters from *SF Commentary,* including contributions by Turner, Gillespie, Lem, and Dick himself.

Greenberg, Martin Harry, and Joseph D. Olander, eds. *Philip K. Dick.* Writers of the 21st Century Series. New York: Taplinger, 1983. Includes solid essays by Disch, Warrick, Warren, Hayles, Suvin, Bishop, and others.

Pierce, Hazel. *Philip K. Dick.* Mercer Island, Wash.: Starmont House, 1982. Overview of major works, heavy on plot summary.

Rickman, Gregg. *Philip K. Dick: A Life.* Long Beach, Calif.: Fragments West/ Valentine Press, 1988. Biography based on many interviews with Dick and the people who knew him.

———. *Philip K. Dick: In His Own Words.* Long Beach, Calif.: Fragments West/Valentine Press, 1984. Interviews with Dick focusing on his works.

———. *Philip K. Dick: The Last Testament.* Long Beach, Calif.: Fragments West/Valentine Press, 1985. Interviews with Dick on his religious and philosophical ideas.

Robinson, Kim Stanley. *The Novels of Philip K. Dick.* Ann Arbor, Mich.: UMI Research Press, 1984. Stimulating survey of Dick's science fiction novels by one of the best of younger science-fiction writers. Emphasis on narrative structure and fictional techniques.

Taylor, Angus. *Philip K. Dick and the Umbrella of Light.* Baltimore, Md.: T-K Graphics, 1975. Deft synthesis of major themes in Dick's novels of the 1960s.

Warrick, Patricia S. *Mind in Motion: The Fiction of Philip K. Dick.* Carbondale: Southern Illinois University Press, 1987. In-depth studies of eight major Dick novels by an excellent critic.

Williams, Paul. *Only Apparently Real: The World of Philip K. Dick.* New York: Arbor House, 1986. Fascinating interview-based book focusing on Dick's experiences in the 1970s.

3. Interviews

Apel, D. Scott, and Kevin Briggs. "An Interview with Philip K. Dick." *Philip K. Dick Society Newsletter,* no. 5 (December 1984), 5–7, and no. 6 (April 1985), 1–2, 11–14. Discusses backgrounds of several of his novels and what it means to be human.

Boonstra, John. "TZ Interview: Philip K. Dick." *Twilight Zone,* June 1982, 47–52. Touches on the Valis trilogy and *Blade Runner.*

————. "Philip K. Dick." *Patchin Review,* no. 5 (October-December 1982), 2–6. On *Timothy Archer, Blade Runner,* and the zeitgeist.

Cain, George, and Dana Longo. "Philip K. Dick: Confessions of a SF Artist. . . ." *Denver Clarion,* 23 October 1980, 2. Includes discussion of Dick's religious ideas.

Cover, Arthur Byron. "Vertex Interviews Philip K. Dick." *Vertex* 1 (February 1974):34–37, 96–98. Talk of drugs, Taoism.

DePrez, Daniel. "An Interview with Philip K. Dick." *Science Fiction Review* 5 (August 1976): 6–12. Entertaining, wide-ranging interview including background for *A Scanner Darkly* and *Valis.*

[Hodel, Mike]. "The Mainstream That Through the Ghetto Flows: An Interview with Philip K. Dick." *Missouri Review* 7, 2 (1984):164–85. Spirited 1976 interview emphasizing the publishing business and other SF writers.

"Interview with Philip K. Dick." In *Reflections of the Future: Laboratory Manual,* by Russell Hill, 57–58. Lexington, Mass.: Ginn & Co., 1975. Interview with high school students about "Roog."

[Interview with Philip K. Dick.] *Slash* 3, 5 (May 1980):37–38. Mostly on politics.

Lupoff, Richard A. "A Conversation with Philip K. Dick." *Science Fiction Eye,* no. 2 (August 1987). Covers Dick's writing career in the 1950s.

Mallardi, Bill, and Bill Bowers. *The Double: Bill Symposium.* Akron, Ohio: D:B Press, 1969. Includes Dick's written answers to eleven questions about the writing of science fiction.

Platt, Charles. "Philip K. Dick." In *Dream Makers: The Uncommon People Who Write Science Fiction,* 145–58. New York: Berkley, 1980. Lively interview bringing Dick to life in all his unconventional splendor.

Reynolds, J. B. "The PKDS Interview with Tessa B. Dick (and Christopher Dick)." *Philip K. Dick Society Newsletter,* no. 13 (February 1987), 2–9. Interesting background for the Valis years.

Van Hise, James. "Philip K. Dick on *Blade Runner.*" *Starlog,* no. 55 (February 1982), 19–22. Details of the problems with the film adaptation of *Do Androids Dream of Electric Sheep?*

Vitale, Joe. "The Worlds of Philip K. Dick: An Interview with America's
    Most Brilliant Science-Fiction Writer." *The Aquarian,* 11/18 October
    1978, 9–10. Discusses philosophical and literary influences.
Watson, Andy. "The PKDS Interview with K. W. Jeter." *Philip K. Dick
    Society Newsletter,* no. 5 (Dec. 1984), 1–2, 10–16.
————. "The PKDS Interview with Tim Powers and James P. Blaylock."
    *Philip K. Dick Society Newsletter,* no. 8 (September 1985), 3–5, 12–13.
    Both of these interviews provide insights and anecdotes from young writ-
    ers who were close to Dick.
Williams, Paul. "Philip K. Dick in Conversation with Paul Williams
    Oct/Nov 1974." *Philip K. Dick Society Newsletter,* no. 9/10, January 1986.
    Sound recording. On, among other things, *Now Wait for Last Year,* Mus-
    solini, Jung, and multiple points of view in narration.
————. "The True Stories of Philip K. Dick." *Rolling Stone,* 6 November
    1975, 45 ff. Influential interview/essay that contributed to rediscovery of
    Dick in the 1970s, including biographical background and an inspired
    appreciation.

4. Articles
Abrash, Merritt. "Elusive Utopias: Societies as Mechanisms in the Early Fic-
    tion of Philip K. Dick." In *Clockwork Worlds: Mechanized Environments in
    SF,* edited by Richard D. Erlich and Thomas P. Dunn, 115–23. Westport
    and London: Greenwood, 1983. The lack of utopian vision in the socie-
    ties of Dick's early fiction.
————. "Sparring with the Universe: Heroism and Futility in Philip K.
    Dick's Protagonists." *Extrapolation* 27 (Summer 1986): 116–22. A view
    of the Dickian hero as a decent man in an incomprehensible universe.
Aldiss, Brian W. "Dick's Maledictory Web." In *Philip K. Dick,* edited by
    Greenberg and Olander, 97–104. Revised from *Science-Fiction Studies* 2
    (March 1975):42–47. The "building blocks" of *Martian Time-Slip.*
————. "Philip K. Dick: A Whole New Can of Worms." *Foundation,* no. 26
    (October 1982), 11–14. Tribute to Dick's overall contribution: a "schiz-
    oid portrait of the coming age."
Astle, Richard. "*Martian Time-Slip.*" In *Survey of Science Fiction Literature,* ed-
    ited by Frank N. Magill, 3:1357–61. Englewood Cliffs, N.J.: Salem
    Press, 1979. How the schizophrenic process pervades the whole novel.
Bertrand, Frank C. "Encounters with Reality: P. K. Dick's *A Scanner Darkly.*"
    *Philosophical Speculations,* no. 1 (March 1981), 12–17. Emphasizes Dick's
    conception of reality with respect to the ideas of Teilhard de Chardin.
————. "Kant's 'Noumenal Self' and Doppelganger in P. K. Dick's *A Scanner
    Darkly.*" *Philosophical Speculations,* no. 2 (Summer 1981), 69-80. The
    split personality of Arctor/Fred as reflecting Kant's ideas of the phenom-
    enal and noumenal selves.

Bishop, Michael. "In Pursuit of *Ubik.*" In *Philip K. Dick,* edited by Greenberg and Olander, 137–47. Very original interpretation of the puzzles of *Ubik.*

Bray, Mary Kay. "Mandalic Activism: An Approach to Structure, Theme, and Tone in Four Novels by Philip K. Dick." *Extrapolation* 21 (Summer 1980):146–57. The principle of macrocosm and microcosm in *Now Wait for Last Year, Ubik, A Maze of Death,* and *Flow My Tears, the Policeman Said.*

Burden, Brian J. "Philip K. Dick and Metaphysics of American Politics" *Foundation,* no. 26 (October 1982), 41–46. Dick's early fiction as reflecting the political climate of the 1950s and anticipating the 1960s.

Chapman, Edgar L. "*Dr. Bloodmoney.*" In *Survey of Science Fiction Literature,* edited by Frank N. Magill, 2:564–68. Englewood Cliffs, N.J.: Salem Press, 1979. Somewhat lukewarm assessment, claiming weak portrayal of Bluthgeld.

Disch, Thomas M. "In the Mold of 1964: An Afterword." In *The Penultimate Truth.* New York: Bluejay Books, 1984. *The Penultimate Truth* as a reflection of the political climate of the early 1960s.

———. "Toward the Transcendent: An Introduction to *Solar Lottery* and Other Works." In *Philip K. Dick,* edited by Greenberg and Olander, 13–25. Thoughtful evaluation of Dick's first published novel.

Fitting, Peter. "*Ubik*: The Deconstruction of Bourgeois SF." In *Philip K. Dick,* edited by Greenberg and Olander, 149–59, and *Science-Fiction Studies* 2 (March 1975):47–54. *Ubik* as a critique and challenge of fictional and science-fictional conventions.

———. "Reality as Ideological Construct: A Reading of Five Novels by Philip K. Dick." *Science-Fiction Studies* 10 (July 1983):219–36. An ideological approach to the theme of breakthrough to a higher reality, with reference to sociopolitical context.

Freedman, Carl. "Towards a Theory of Paranoia: The Science Fiction of Philip K. Dick." *Science-Fiction Studies* 11 (March 1984):15–24. Dick's protagonists as paranoiac antiheroes; a Marxist/Lacanian reading.

Frenkel, James. Afterword to *Dr. Bloodmoney.* New York: Bluejay Books, 1985. The novel as morality play.

Frisch, Adam J. "Language Fragmentation in Recent Science-Fiction Novels." In *The Intersection of Science Fiction and Philosophy: Critical Studies,* edited by Robert E. Meyers, 147–58. Westport, Conn.: Greenwood Press, 1983. Discusses *A Scanner Darkly* in terms of communication breakdown within a character's brain.

Galbreath, Robert. "Redemption and Doubt in Philip K. Dick's Valis Trilogy." *Extrapolation* 24 (Summer 1983):105–15. Discusses unifying moral and religious themes in Dick's final three novels.

———. "Salvation-Knowledge: Ironic Gnosticism in *Valis* and *The Flight to Lucifer.*" In *Science-Fiction Dialogues,* edited by Gary Wolfe, 115–32. Chicago: Academy Chicago, 1982. Argues that Dick uses Gnostic metaphysics while critiquing it; compares *VALIS* with a novel by Harold Bloom.

Gillespie, Bruce. "*The Best of Philip K. Dick*." In *Survey of Science Fiction Literature*, edited by Frank N. Magill, 2:196–201. Englewood Cliffs, N.J.: Salem Press, 1979. Survey of stories in Dick's "Best of" collection.

————. "Contradictions." *SF Commentary*, no. 4 (July 1969), 55–69.

————. "Mad, Mad Worlds: Seven Novels of Philip K. Dick." *SF Commentary*, no. 1 (January 1969), 36–52.

————. "The Real Thing." *SF Commentary*, no. 9 (February 1970), 11–25. This and the previous two entries are long reviews of Dick's 1960s novels, focusing on artistic successes and problems. Reprinted in *Philip K. Dick: Electric Shepherd*, edited by Bruce Gillespie.

Hartwell, David. Introduction to *Counter-Clock World*. Boston: Gregg Press, 1979. Defends the novels as a radical experiment with "considerable depth and richness."

Hayles, N. B. "Metaphysics and Metafiction in *The Man in the High Castle*." In *Philip K. Dick*, edited by Greenberg and Olander, 53–72. Fine essay on Dick's metafictional "leap from morality to ontology."

Jameson, Fredric. "After Armageddon: Character Systems in *Dr. Bloodmoney*." *Science-Fiction Studies* 2 (March 1975):31–42. Complex and thought-provoking schematization of character relationships.

Kaveny, Philip E. "From Pessimism to Sentimentality: *Do Androids Dream of Electric Sheep* Becomes *Blade Runner*." In *Patterns of the Fantastic II*, edited by Donald M. Hassler, 77–80. Mercer Island, Wash.: Starmont House, 1985. Thinks that the movie substituted sentimentality for the introspection of the novel.

Kerman, Judith B. "Private Eye: A Semiotic Comparison of the Film *Blade Runner* and the Book *Do Androids Dream of Electric Sheep*." In *Patterns of the Fantastic II*, edited by Donald M. Hassler, 69–75. Mercer Island, Wash.: Starmont House, 1985. Argues that the film is a richer, more compelling experience than the novel.

Kinney, Jay. "The Mysterious Revelations of Philip K. Dick." *Gnosis*, no. 1 (Fall/Winter 1985), 6–11. Useful for background of the "Exegesis" and *VALIS*.

Knight, Damon. *In Search of Wonder*. 2d ed., 228–35. Chicago: Advent, 1967. This seminal critical work includes a critique of Dick's early novels.

Le Guin, Ursula K. "Science Fiction as Prophesy [sic]." *New Republic*, 30 October 1976, 33–34. Eloquent appeal to consider Dick as a major writer.

Lem, Stanislaw. "Philip K. Dick: A Visionary among the Charlatans." *Science-Fiction Studies* 2 (March 1975):54–67.

————. "Science Fiction: A Hopeless Case—with Exceptions." *SF Commentary,* no. 35/36/37, 7–36. The important Polish novelist praises Dick as essentially the only American science fiction writer of importance, but not without qualifications.

Lupoff, Richard. "The Realities of Philip K. Dick." *Starship,* Summer 1979, 29–33. Comments on stories in *A Handful of Darkness;* includes quotations from Dick on his short story writing.

Mackey, Douglas A. "*Eye in the Sky.*" In *Survey of Science Fiction Literature,* edited by Frank N. Magill, 2:744–48. Englewood Cliffs, N.J.: Salem Press, 1979. The relativity of the subjective worlds in the novel.

————. "Science Fiction and Gnosticism." *Missouri Review* 7, 2 (1984), 112–20. Gnostic themes in Dick and other writers.

Malmgren, Carl D. "Philip Dick's *Man in the High Castle* and the Nature of Science-Fictional Worlds." In *Bridges to Science Fiction,* edited by George E. Slusser, George R. Guffey, and Mark Rose, 120–30. Carbondale: Southern Illinois University Press, 1980. On Dick's metafictional revelation of reality as subjective.

Malzberg, Barry. Afterword to *Clans of the Alphane Moon.* New York: Bluejay Books, 1984. Portrays Dick as struggling against literary and economic constraints of the science-fiction field.

McNelly, Willis E. "*The Man in the High Castle.*" In *Survey of Science Fiction Literature,* edited by Frank N. Magill, 3:1323–27. Englewood Cliffs, N.J.: Salem Press, 1979. Emphasizes Juliana as representing the fullness of the Tao.

Miesel, Sandra. Introduction to *Eye in the Sky.* Boston: Gregg Press, 1979. Best analysis of Dick's first major novel.

Milicia, Joseph. Introduction to *The Man in the High Castle.* Boston: Gregg Press, 1979. Very useful, detailed analysis including quotations from Dick's letters.

Neilson, Keith. "Philip K. Dick." In *Critical Survey of Short Fiction,* edited by Frank N. Magill, 1260–66. Englewood Cliffs, N.J.: Salem Press, 1981. Survey of Dick's major short stories.

————. "*Ubik.*" In *Survey of Science Fiction Literature,* edited by Frank N. Magill, 5:2350–55. Englewood Cliffs, N.J.: Salem Press, 1979. *Ubik* as metaphysical detective story.

Nicholls, Peter. "Philip K. Dick: A Cowardly Memoir." *Foundation,* no. 26 (October 1982), 5–10. One view of Dick's enigmatic personality.

Pagetti, Carlo. "Dick and Meta-SF." *Science-Fiction Studies* 2 (1975):24–31. Sees Dick's SF as fiction that transcends the limitations of its genre.

Pierce, Hazel. "*Flow My Teams, the Policeman Said.*" In *Survey of Science Fiction Literature,* edited by Frank N. Magill, 2:797–801. Englewood Cliffs, N.J.: Salem Press, 1979. Sees characters in the novels as attempting to balance inner and outer realities.

————. "Philip K. Dick's Political Dreams." In *Philip K. Dick,* edited by Greenberg and Olander, 105–35. The exercise of power in Dick's early 1960s novels.

Platt, Charles. Introduction to *The Zap Gun.* Boston: Gregg Press, 1979. Focuses on the characters of the novel and the background of its composition.

Silverberg, Robert. Introduction to *Clans of the Alphane Moon.* Boston: Gregg Press, 1979. Includes interesting comments on Dick's style.

Simons, John L. "The Power of Small Things in Philip K. Dick's *The Man in the High Castle.*" *Rocky Mountain Review* 39 (1985):261–75. Close reading with emphasis on the theme of smallness and its importance in Dick's philosophy.

Spinrad, Norman. Introduction to *Dr. Bloodmoney.* Boston: Gregg Press, 1977. Focuses on "the multiplexity of reality" as "the core of Dick's work."

Stableford, Brian. "*The Three Stigmata of Palmer Eldritch.*" In *Survey of Science Fiction Literature,* edited by Frank N. Magill, 5:2269–73. Englewood Cliffs, N.J.: Salem Press, 1979. Sees incongruities in plot as heightening the sense of dislocation.

Stathis, Louis. Afterword to *Time out of Joint.* New York: Bluejay Books, 1984.

————. Introduction to *Time out of Joint.* Boston: Gregg Press, 1979. Along with Afterword cited above, contains valuable background on the writing of this novel.

Stewart, Bhob. "Do Replicants Dream of Philip K. Dick?" *Comics Journal,* no. 76 (October 1982), 121–34. Lively account of Dick's career, emphasizing his links to the comics and comics illustrators.

Strick, Philip. "Philip K. Dick and the Movies." *Foundation,* no. 26 (October 1982), 15–21. Focuses on the relationship of *Do Androids Dream of Electric Sheep?* and *Blade Runner.*

Suvin, Darko. "Artifice as Refuge and World View: Philip K. Dick's Foci." In *Philip K. Dick,* edited by Greenberg and Olander, 73–95. Revised from *Science-Fiction Studies* 2 (March 1975):8–22. An influential critic praises Dick's political themes and multifoci technique and denigrates his ontological interests.

Taylor, Angus. "Can God Fly? Can He Hold Out His Arms and Fly?—The Fiction of Philip K. Dick." *Foundation,* no. 4 (July 1973), 32–47. An overview of major themes in Dick.

————. "The Politics of Space, Time and Entropy." *Foundation* (June 1976), 34–44. Identifies Dick's and Ursula Le Guin's political values as similar but arrived at from different perspectives.

Thurston, Robert. Introduction to *The Game-Players of Titan.* Boston: Gregg Press, 1979. Lucid explanation of a complex, underappreciated novel.

Turner, George. "Philip K. Dick by 1975: Flow My Tears, the Policeman Said." In *Philip K. Dick: Electric Shepherd,* edited by Bruce Gillespie, 94–

100. Rejects notion of Dick as a "fine" writer; criticizes hasty style, non-realistic background, and vague characterization.

Wagner, Jeff. "In the World He Was Writing About: The Life of Philip K. Dick." *Foundation*, no. 34 (Autumn 1985), 69–96. The first detailed exposition of the major events of Dick's life.

Warren, Eugene. "The Search for Absolutes." In *Philip K. Dick*, edited by Greenberg and Olander, 161–88. Brilliant synthesis of Dick's political and religious themes, based on the search for absolute reality.

Warrick, Patricia S. "The Encounter of Taoism and Fascism in *The Man in the High Castle*. In *Philip K. Dick*, edited by Greenberg and Olander, 27–52. Convincing thematic approach to a major novel.

————. "The Labyrinthian Process of the Artificial: Philip K. Dick's Androids and Mechanical Constructs." *Extrapolation* 20 (Summer 1979):133–53. In *Philip K. Dick*, edited by Greenberg and Olander, 189–214. Thorough, skilled exploration of the theme of the mechanical vs. the human in a number of major Dick novels and stories.

————. "Philip K. Dick's Answers to the Eternal Riddles." In *The Transcendent Adventure: Studies of Religion in Science-Fiction/Fantasy*, edited by Robert Reilly, 107–26. Westport, Conn.: Greenwood Press, 1985.

Watson, Ian. "Le Guin's *Lathe of Heaven* and the Role of Dick: The False Reality as Mediator." *Science-Fiction Studies* 2 (March 1975): 67–75. The influence on Le Guin of the Dickian mode of portraying false reality-constructs.

Williams, Paul. Introduction to *Confessions of a Crap Artist*. Glen Ellen, Calif.: Entwhistle Books, 1975. Includes valuable background and quotes from Dick on the writing of his best mainstream novel.

————. Introduction to *The Three Stigmata of Palmer Eldritch*. Boston: Gregg Press, 1979. Essential, well-informed essay on the background of Dick's most fascinating novel.

Wingrove, David. "Understanding the Grasshopper: Leitmotifs and the Moral Dilemma in the Novels of Philip K. Dick." *Foundation*, no. 26 (October 1982), 21–40. A fine synthesis of Dick's metaphors, drawing on many novels, arriving at his "essential moral purpose."

Wolk, Anthony. "The Sunstruck Forest: A Guide to the Short Fiction of Philip K. Dick." *Foundation*, no. 18 (January 1980), 19–33. Surveys themes such as empathy and reality in a broad range of stories, and relates them to the novels.

5. Periodical

*The Philip K. Dick Society Newsletter.* 1983-   . Published by the Philip K. Dick Society, Box 611, Glen Ellen, California 95442. Indispensable, well-edited newsletter featuring extracts from Dick's unpublished writings, news of forthcoming publications by and about Dick, photos, interviews, and letters.

# Index

Ace Books, 14, 16, 17, 22, 24, 26, 29,
    82, 87, 101
Ahriman, 15, 52
Ahura Mazda, 15
*Amazing Stories*, 52
Anderson, Poul, 9
Anima, 16, 25, 28, 32, 34, 41, 45, 53,
    63, 79, 85, 86, 90, 98, 105, 108,
    124, *129*
*Anokhi*, 114, 125, 126
Arctor, Bob (*A Scanner Darkly*), 110–
    11, 115
Armaiti, 16
Asklepios, 119
Atman, 95
Augustine, St., 86

Ballantine Books, 55
Bantam Books, 115
Being, 76, 97
Berkeley, Bishop, 28
Berkeley (California), 1, 2, 115
Berkley Books, 82
Bester, Alfred: *The Demolished Man*,
    16–17
Bible, 11, 110, 114, 122
Bishop, Michael, 94
*Blade Runner* (film), 5, 88
Blake, William, 5
Bloode's text, Dr. (*The Unteleported
    Man*), *84*, 98
Bloom, Molly, 37, 127
Bluthgeld, Bruno (*Dr. Bloodmoney*), 20,
    *59–60*, 62, 65, 66, 113
Boethius, 86
Bohm, David, 96
Bonner, Liz (*Puttering About in a Small
    Land*), *37–38*, 41
Boucher, Anthony, 1
Brown, Fredric: *What Mad Universe*, 22
Buckman, Alys (*Flow My Tears*), 20, 66,
    *103–5*, 123

Buddhism, 76, 113, 114, 119

Candide, 75
Capitalism, 24, 128
*Caritas*, 70
Christ, 95, 99, 121
Christianity, 16, 75–76, 87, 100, 112,
    114, 116, 125, 127
Communism, 24, 25, 96, 99, 107
Conley, Pat (*Ubik*), 10, 47–49, 52
Corn King, 116
Cyclops, 119

Dante, 119; *Divine Comedy*, 86, 126
Davies, Paul, 96
Del Rey, Judy-Lynn, 109
Del Rey Books, 109
Demiurge, 76, 107
Dick, Anne Rubenstein, 2
Dick, Kleo Apostolides, 2, 3
Dick, Nancy Hackett, 4, 125
Dick, Philip K.
    aliens in, 6, 7, 8, 12, 57, 62–64, 67,
        70, 71, 83, 87, 102–3, 107, 128;
    alternate worlds in, 22, 29, 47, 50–
        51, 69, 71, 83, 104–5, 115;
    androids and simulacra in, 18, 52–
        54, 57, 64, 65, 66, 87, 88–92, 129;
    charismatic leader-figure in, 20, 29,
        32–33, 65, 67–68, 81, 85; comedy
    and humor in, 22, 42, 62, 64, 69,
        72, 77, 80, 88; "dark-haired girl" in,
        10, 25, 28, 30, 108–9, 120, 129;
    drugs in, 4, 58, 63, 67, 72–75, 100,
        103, 107, 109–11, 120, 128; early
    life, 1; earnings, 3; empathy in, 67,
        70, 79, 89–90; evil gods in, 7, 8,
        15, 23, 48, 57, 60, 74–77, 93, 107,
        112, 118; evolution of consciousness
    in, 2, 12, 14, 19, 65, 73–74, 77,
        83, 101, 103, 114, 131; interest in

music, 1, 34, 105; literary influences on, 1, 2, 16–17; logical paradox in, 84, 95–96, 121; mainstream novels of, 2–3, 19, 26, *31–46*, 52, 124, 129–30; male-female relationships in, 21, 37–38, 42, 43–45, 68, 69, 79, 85–86, 98, 104; media manipulation in, 9, 13, 25, 26, 64, 65, 66, 68, 77–78, 79–80; mental instability of, 1, 4, 5; multifocal narration in, 32, 40, 42, 47, 55, 59, 64, 72, 128; on the nature of reality, 12–13, 14, 24, 28–29, 51, 68, 70, 75, 77, 88, 92, 95–96; paranoia in, 5, 7, 8, 11, 14, 24, 28, 45, 56, 60, 62, 65, 70, 110; policeman figure in, 21, 90, 91, 105, 110; personality, 5; politics in, 19, 77–78, 79, 83, 101; pots and pottery in, 77, 97, 98, 104, 105–6, 112; psi powers in, 10, 13, 21, 63, 72, 78, 92, 102, 128; randomness and chance in, 17, 18, 49, 63; reality breakdown in, 17, 23, 25–26, 27, 56, 106–7; religion in, 89–90, 99–100; religious beliefs of, 3, 131; robots and intelligent machines in, 9, 11, 12, 62, 68–69, 79, 89, 91; schizophrenia in, 53–59, 65, 70, 87, 91, 104, 110–11, 116; and the subjectivity of "objective" reality, 2, 20, 27–29, 51, 70, 74, 92, 104, 106–7, 118, 122–23, 131; time paradoxes in, 29, 67–68, 83, 85, 86, 124; transcendence in, 28, 86–76, 88, 92, 118, 121; visionary experiences of, 3, 4, 117; on women, 44–45, 108, 128–29

WORKS—NOVELS:
*Blade Runner*. See *Do Androids Dream of Electric Sheep?*
*Broken Bubble, The*, 2, 31, 35–36
*Clans of the Alphane Moon*, 3, 69–71, 103
*Confessions of a Crap Artist*, 2, 22, 31, 40–42, 129
*Cosmic Puppets, The*, 2, 14–16, 19, 27, 33, 52, 113

*Counter-Clock World*, 3, 21, 84–87, 92, 106, 129
*Crack in Space, The*, 3, 71–72, 83, 106
*Deus Irae*, 111–13, 115
*Divine Invasion, The*, 4, 5, 10, 15, 18, 122–24, 126, 129
*Do Androids Dream of Electric Sheep?*, 3, 5, 11, 21, 88–92, 100, 106, 129
*Dr. Bloodmoney*, 2, 20, 55, 59–62, 65, 112–13, 129
*Dr. Futurity*, 2, 29–30, 80
*Eye in the Sky*, 2, 13, 14, 22–24, 29, 60, 76, 99, 103, 129
*Flow My Tears, the Policeman Said*, 3, 13, 20, 24, 66, 103–6, 129
*Galactic Pot-Healer*, 3, 96–99, 116, 129
*Game-Players of Titan, The*, 3, 55, 62–64, 87, 130
*Ganymede Takeover, The*, 3, 87–88
*Gather Yourselves Together*, 2, 31, 33
*Humpty Dumpty in Oakland*, 2, 31, 45–46
*In Milton Lumky Territory*, 2, 31, 38–40
*Lies, Inc.* See *Unteleported Man*
*Man in the High Castle, The*, 3, 47–52, 62, 95, 100, 119, 129
*Man Who Japed, The*, 2, 9, 22, 22–24, 116
*Man Whose Teeth Were All Exactly Alike, The*, 2, 31, 42–45, 71, 80
*Martian Time-Slip*, 3, 10, 20, 37, 53, 55–59, 62, 63, 66, 74, 82, 129
*Mary and the Giant*, 2, 31, 34–35
*Maze of Death, A*, 3, 15, 26, 99–101
*Nicholas and the Higs*, 31
*Now Wait for Last Year*, 3, 33, 67–69, 79, 81, 101, 116, 130
*Our Friends from Frolix*, 3, 8, 101–3
*Owl in Daylight, The*, 86, 126
*Penultimate Truth, The*, 3, 9, 55, 77, 79–81, 82, 83, 101
*Pilgrim on the Hill*, 31
*Puttering About in a Small Land*, 2, 31, 36–38, 41

*Radio Free Albemuth*, 4, *115–17*, 119, 129
*Return to Lilliput*, 1
*Scanner Darkly, A*, 4, 21, 67, 107, *109–11*, 115, 124, 129
*Simulacra, The*, 3, 9, 36, 55, *64–67*, 68, 71, 83, 101, 106, 130
*Solar Lottery*, 2, 6, 14, *16–19*, 24, 32, 63
*Three Stigmata of Palmer Eldritch, The*, 3, 7, 13, 24, 53, 55, 57, 64, 66, 67, *72–77*, 82, 83, 90, 100, 101, 106, 107, 113, 118, 122, 129
*Time for George Stavros, A*, 31
*Time out of Joint*, 2, 9, 22, *26–29*, 129
*Transmigration of Timothy Archer, The*, 4, *124–27*, 129
*Ubik*, 3, 10, 15, 24, 26, 37, 61, *92–96*, 100, 103, 106, 107, 113, 129
*Unteleported Man, The*, 3, 67, 71, *82–84*, 98
*VALIS*, 4, 5, 10, 26, 76, 95, 115, 116, *117–21*, 122, 124, 129, 131
*Voice from the Street*, 2, 31, *32–33*
*Vulcan's Hammer*, 2, 29, *30*
*We Can Build You*, 3, *52–55*, 65, 90–91, 101, 130
*World Jones Made, The*, 2, *19–22*
*Zap Gun, The*, 3, *77–79*, 80, 84, 130

WORKS—NON-FICTION
"Dark-Haired Girl, The," *108–9*
"Evolution of a Vital Love, The," 129
"Exegesis," 4, *113–14*, 115, 118, 119
"Man, Android and Machine," 90

WORKS—SHORT FICTION
"A. Lincoln, Simulacrum," 52
"Adjustment Team," *12–13*
"All We Marsmen," 55
"Autofac," 6, 9
"Beyond Lies the Door," 7
"Beyond Lies the Wub," 6
"Cantata 140," 71, 106
"Chromium Fence, The," 10
"Colony," 6, 8
"Commuter, The," 14

"Cookie Lady, The," 7
"Cosmic Poachers, The," *7–8*
"Days of Perky Pat, The," 106
"Defenders, The," 9, 80
"Electric Ant, The," 106
"Exhibit Piece," 14
"Expendable," 8
"Explorers We," 12
"Fair Game," 7
"Faith of Our Fathers," 18, 57, 76, 107
"Father-Thing, The," 12
"Foster, You're Dead," 8
"Glass of Darkness, A," 15
"Golden Man, The," 10
"Great C, The," 9, 112
"Hanging Stranger, The," 8
"Hood Maker, The," 10
"Human Is," 12
"Impostor," 6, 11
"King of the Elves, The," 6
"Last of the Masters, The," 9
"Little Black Box, The," 106
"Little Movement, The," 9
"Martians Come in Clouds," 7
"Misadjustment," 13
"Mold of Yancy, The," 9, 80
"Mr. Spaceship," 11
"Nanny," 8
"Novelty Act," 106
"Paycheck," 17
"Planet for Transients," 112
"Precious Artifact," 106
"Prominent Author," 11
"Retreat Syndrome," 106
"Roog," 1, 6
"Sales Pitch," 9
"Second Variety," 6, 12, 30
"Service Call," 9
"Shell Game," 14
"Skull, The," 11
"Small Town," 13
"Strange Eden," *6–7*
"Time Pawn," 29
"Tony and the Beetles," 7
"Trouble with Bubbles, The," 11
"Unreconstructed M, The," 80
"Upon the Dull Earth," 6, 11
"Variable Man, The," 10, 63

"Waterspider," 9
"We Can Remember It for You
    Wholesale," 106
"What the Dead Men Say," 106
"World of Talent, A," 10
"World She Wanted, The," 13
"Your Appointment Will Be
    Yesterday," 106

Dick, Tessa Busby, 4, 108
Dionysian possession, 120
Disch, Thomas M., 17
Donne, John, 91
Dos Passos, John, 1
Doubleday, 88
Dowland, John, 105, 123–24
Dreiser, Theodore, 1
Dystopia, 17, 30, 59, 65, 96

Eckehart, Miester, 119
Eden, 73
Eldritch, Palmer (*The Three Stigmata of
    Palmer Eldritch*), 3, 48, 74–77, 83,
    90, 93, 102, 107, 123
Elizabethan songs, 105
Ellison, Harlan: *Dangerous Visions,* 107
Entropy, 15, 17, 18, 21, 28, 55, 61,
    92, 93, 95, 99
Epicureanism, 87
Episcopalianism, 3–4
Erigena, John Scotus, 86
Escher, M. C., 95
Existential psychology, 2, 22

Fall of Man, 7, 75, 114, 116
*Fantastic,* 82
Faust, 75, 98, 114
FBI, 12
Febbs, Surley G. (*The Zap Gun*), 78–79,
    84
Feminine, archetypal, 16, 37, 49, 53,
    54–55
Fitting, Peter, 94
Flaubert, Gustave, 1
Frauenzimmer, Pris (*We Can Build You*),
    52–55, 65, 90–91, 101
Freud, Sigmund, 48

Glimmung, the (*Galactic Pot-Healer*),
    97–99, 116
Gnosticism, 30, 75–77, 93, 100, 107,
    114, 118, 120, 122, 131
God, 48, 57, 76–77, 92, 97, 99–100,
    102–3, 107, 114, 116, 118, 119,
    122, 123, 125, 126
Goethe, 119
Gollancz, Victor, 82, 83
*Grasshopper Lies Heavy, The,* 50–51, 119
Great Mother (archetype), 7, 16, 54, 65

Harrington, Hoppy (*Dr. Bloodmoney*),
    60–61, 65, 113
Hartwell, David, 87
Hayles, N. B., 51
Heinlein, Robert A., 130
Hemingway, Ernest, 1
Heraclitus, 119, 123
Herbert, Frank, 130
Hermes Trismegistos, 119
Hinduism, 76
Hitler, Adolf, 20
Hofstadter, Douglas: *Godel, Escher, Bach,*
    96, 121
Holomovement, 96
Holy Grail, 118
Hugo Award, 3, 47
Hurst, Mark, 115

*I Ching,* 47, 49–50, 51
Idealism, philosophic, 28
*Idois kosmos,* 22–23, 24, 27, 51, 79, 95,
    96, 99, 101, 106, 109
Ikhnaton, 119
Individuation, 7, 98
Isidore, Jack (*Confessions of a Crap
    Artist*), 40–42, 78
Isidore of Seville, 41

Jameson, Fredric, 59
John W. Campbell Award, 3
Jory (*Ubik*), 61, 93, 123
Joyce, James, 1; *Ulysses,* 37, 127
Judaic esotericism, 123
Jung, C. G., 2, 6, 23, 25, 30, 32, 44,
    48, 63, 96, 98, 100

Kabbalah, 114, 123
Kennedys, the, 116, 125
King, Martin Luther, 116, 125
Knight, Damon: *In Search of Wonder*, 24
*Koinos kosmos*, 22–23, 27, 51, 95, 96,
    101, 109
Kott, Arnie (*Martian Time-Slip*), 55–56,
    57–58, 74
Kubrick, Stanley: *Dr. Strangelove*, 59;
    *2001: A Space Odyssey*, 30

Laing, R. D.: *The Politics of Experience*,
    57
Lao-tzu, 119
Leary, Timothy, 73
Le Guin, Ursula K., 49, 129, 130
Lem, Stanislaw, 130
Lindsay, David: *A Voyage to Arcturus*,
    122
Lippincott, 26
Logos, 95, 113, 118
Loman, Willy, 38
LSD, 73, 83, 100
Lucretius, 87

McCarthy, Joseph, 24
*Magazine of Fantasy and Science Fiction*, 1,
    71
Maya, 24, 75, 77, 95, 96, 120, 129
Metafiction, 94, 121, 131
Miller, Arthur: *Death of a Salesman*, 38
Molinari, Gino (*Now Wait for Last Year*),
    33, 67–69, 81
Moral Majority, 25, 116
Mussolini, Benito, 68

Nag Hammadi gospels, 119
Nazism, 10, 47–49
Nelson, Ray, 87
Neoplatonism, 114
Nixon, Richard, 115

Odysseus, 6
Ormazd, 15, 52
Orphism, 114

Paraclete, 71
Parmenides, 119

Paul, St., 110
Pauli, Wolfgang, 63
*Peter Pan*, 54
*Philip K. Dick Society Newsletter*, 83
Pierce, Hazel, 95
Pike, James A., 125
Plato, 80, 92, 106, 119
Puritans, 25
Pyramid Books, 77

Quantum theory, 96

Reincarnation, 93
Relativity, general, 96
Rickman, Gregg, 42, 129
Robinson, Kim Stanley, 38, 59, 67, 94,
    101
Roman Empire, 118
Ronstadt, Linda, 123
Roosevelt, Franklin, 51
Runciter, Glen (*Ubik*), 92, 94, 95, 100
Running Clam, Lord (*Clans of the
    Alphane Moon*), 70, 71, 103

St. Marie, Buffy, 104
Satan, 113–14, 122
*Satellite Science Fiction*, 14
Science fiction: conventions of, 77, 124,
    130; Dick's idea of, 1; in the 1950s
    and 60s, 3
Scott, Ridley, 88
Shadow (archetype), 18, 20, 30, 48, 90,
    98, 105
Shakespeare, William: *The Taming of the
    Shrew*, 44
Shiva, 119
Sladek, John, 82
Solipsism, 13, 58, 60, 87, 104, 128
Spinoza, 54, 119
Stathis, Lou, 28
Steiner, Manfred (*Martian Time-Slip*),
    10, 20, 55–58, 63, 66
"Strange Loop," 96, 121
Superspace, theory of, 96
Suvin, Darko, 59
Swift, Jonathan: "A Modest Proposal,"
    26
Synchronicity, 63

Taoism, 2, 49–50, 51–52
*Tibetan Book of the Dead, The*, 93, 100, 114
Torah, 123

Ubik (*Ubik*), 92–95, 106, 113
Uncertainty principle, 10, 109
*Uncle Tom's Cabin*, 27
Unified field, 92, 93, 96, 106, 109, 131

Valis (*Radio Free Albemuth* and *VALIS*), 4, 113–14, 115, 116, 117, 118, 119
Vance, Jack: *Space Opera*, 77
Van Vogt, A. E., 2; *The World of Null-A*, 16
Vedantism, 16, 129
Vonnegut, Kurt: *Player Piano*, 16

Watson, Ian, 94
White, Ted, 52
Whitman, Walt, 5
Williams, Paul, 5, 72, 102, 103, 129
*Winnie the Pooh*, 54
Wollheim, Donald A., 16, 82
World SF Convention (1963), 47
*Worlds of Tomorrow*, 55
Wright, Richard, 1

Yang and yin, 49–50, 116
Yeats, W. B., 5

Zelazny, Roger, 111–12
Zen Buddhism, 2
Zoroastrianism, 15